# Abortion Politics

# Abortion Politics

*Ziad Munson*

polity

First published in 2018 by Polity Press

Polity Press
65 Bridge Street
Cambridge CB2 1UR, UK

Polity Press
101 Station Landing
Suite 300
Medford, MA 02155, USA

ISBN-13: 978-0-7456-8878-7 (hardback)
ISBN-13: 978-0-7456-8879-4 (paperback)

A catalogue record for this book is available from the British Library.

Library of Congress Cataloging-in-Publication Data
Names: Munson, Ziad W., author.
Title: Abortion politics / Ziad Munson.
Description: Medford, MA : Polity, 2018. | Series: Social movements | Includes bibliographical references and index. |
Identifiers: LCCN 2017050359 (print) | LCCN 2017061152 (ebook) | ISBN 9780745688824 (Epub) | ISBN 9780745688787 (hardback) | ISBN 9780745688794 (paperback)
Subjects: LCSH: Abortion--Political aspects--United States. | Abortion--Government policy--United States. | BISAC: SOCIAL SCIENCE / Sociology / General.
Classification: LCC HQ767.5.U5 (ebook) | LCC HQ767.5.U5 M8596 2018 (print) | DDC 362.1988/80973--dc23
LC record available at https://lccn.loc.gov/2017050359

Typeset in 11 on 13 pt Sabon by
Fakenham Prepress Solutions, Fakenham, Norfolk, NR21 8NN
Printed and bound in Great Britain by Clays Ltd St. Ives PLC

For further information on Polity, visit our website: www.politybooks.com

*To Willow and Elliot*

# Contents

# Acknowledgments

Like so many books, this one has really been a collaborative effort. Conversations with Bayliss Camp, Drew Halfmann, Michael Heaney, Carole Joffe, and Judy Lasker helped me pin down and better articulate some of the major issues raised in the book. A number of students assisted me with research, including Therese Corcoran, Ginger Handley, Natalie Bourman-Karns, and Harvey Nicholson. I also want to thank Lehigh University for the sabbatical during which I laid most of the groundwork for what is written here. I received superb feedback from audiences at several American Sociological Association meetings, the 2016 Comparative–Historical mini-conference in Seattle, the Politics and Protest workshop at CUNY, colloquia in my own department at Lehigh University. Two of the manuscript's anonymous reviewers went above and beyond the call in providing constructive feedback. Thanks to my family, who picked up a lot of the slack I left on the homefront in the final months of putting the manuscript together. Finally, thanks to all of the scholars and activists from whom I've learned so much about this subject over the years. Your work has not only educated me, but inspired me.

# 1

## Introduction

Todd Akin was running to represent Missouri in the US Senate in 2012. A former IBM salesman and steel mill manager, Akin had a quarter century of experience as a politician, serving twelve years in the Missouri House of Representatives, then another twelve years in the US House of Representatives. His campaign for the next step in his long political career, to become a US Senator, was going well. He was running as a conservative Republican in a state that had increasingly voted for Republican candidates in recent elections. He had the strong support of the conservative Tea Party movement and national conservative groups who were spending millions of dollars on his behalf. His opponent, Democrat Claire McCaskill, was considered one of the most vulnerable Senate incumbents in the nation.

Just over two months before the election, Akin was interviewed by local Fox Network affiliate KTVI in St. Louis, during which host Charles Jaco asked him about his abortion views: "What about in the case of rape? Should it be legal or not?" Akin, who had been an activist in the pro-life movement even before his political career, repeated his longstanding position that abortion should be illegal even when a pregnancy is the result of rape. In explaining this position during the interview, he suggested both that some women may falsely claim rape to obtain an abortion and that female physiology made pregnancy as a result of rape extremely rare. "If it's a legitimate rape," Akin said, "the female body has ways ... to shut that whole thing down."

His remarks set off a national firestorm of controversy. Critics, particularly in the pro-choice movement, pointed out, correctly, that the idea women are unlikely to become pregnant as a result of rape is a myth. In fact, the chance of sexual intercourse leading to pregnancy is the same whether the intercourse is the result of rape or consensual sex (Holmes et al. 1996). Moreover, they saw Akin's distinction between legitimate and illegitimate rape claims as perpetuating the dangerous myth that false rape claims are common. Research shows that the majority of rapes are never reported, and only between two percent and eight percent of rape charges are false (Lonsway, Archambault, and Lisak 2009). On the other side, Akin supporters, particularly in the pro-life movement, stood by his candidacy and his specific comments about abortion. Missouri Right to Life, the state affiliation of the National Right to Life Committee (NRLC), repeatedly came to Akin's defense, saying that his words were being "misinterpreted" and that the central point of Akin's remarks was that all unborn children should be protected (Keller 2012). Former Arkansas governor and presidential candidate Mike Huckabee dismissed Akin's words as the "verbal gaffe" of a "principled pro-life advocate" (Holt 2012).

The incident generated national political controversy, as politicians, commentators, pundits, editorial pages, journalists, bloggers, and scholars all debated the implications of Akin's words and the larger debate over abortion. The discussion tied the abortion debate to a myriad different concerns. At issue was medical science, as people debated beliefs about fertility under different conditions. At issue was the problem of sexual assault, as people debated legal definitions and the boundaries of consent. At issue was partisanship, and the implications the incident might have for the fortunes of the two political parties and control of the US Senate. At issue were questions of morality, and whether there were such things as "good" and "bad" abortions. At issue was gender, as the question was raised of whether men and women had an equal right to make policy that impacted reproductive rights. These many debates caused Akin's political fortunes to collapse, and he lost the election to Senator McCaskill, garnering only 39 percent of the vote in the same election that fellow Republican

*Introduction*

Mitt Romney received almost 54 percent of the Missouri vote for President.

A year later, a much different controversy centered on abortion. This time it revolved around the trial of Dr. Kermit Gosnell. Gosnell was a longtime advocate for abortion rights, even before the 1973 Supreme Court decisions legalized the procedure. He opened the Women's Medical Clinic in 1979 to provide abortion and other services in the Philadelphia area, particularly to poor and minority women. Over time, however, his work evolved out of activism and medical practice into a multi-million-dollar business that conducted illegal abortions in unsanitary conditions, provided better care to white women than minority women, and on several occasions killed newborns after they had been delivered alive. The Pennsylvania Department of Health, the Board of Medicine, and the University of Pennsylvania's Presbyterian Medical Center had all seen evidence over the years that something was wrong at Gosnell's clinic, but none of them did much to stop Gosnell's activities or alert authorities (Friedersdorf 2013).

The case once again made abortion the headline of national news and sparked rounds of controversy. Pro-life activists argued that Gosnell and the filthy conditions of his clinic were a window into the reality of abortion nationwide. David O'Steen, the executive director of the NRLC, argued that the case "helped more people realize what abortion is really about" (Associated Press 2013). The case, he said, "once again reminds us that the purpose of each abortion, no matter how it is performed, is to deliberately and brutally take at least one innocent human life" (National Right to Life Committee 2011). Gosnell and his clinic, pro-lifers told the public, were just like every other abortion provider. Pro-life organizations as well as conservative groups also criticized the lack of media coverage of Gosnell and his trial. Republican Congresswoman Marsha Blackburn, from Tennessee, accused the media of a "cover-up" (Viebeck 2013), and many conservative commentators, particularly on blogs and online social media, argued that journalists were deliberately staying away from the trial because it portrayed abortion in a negative light. Pro-choice organizations such as NARAL Pro-Choice America, Planned Parenthood, and the National Organization for Women (NOW) also condemned Dr. Gosnell and his crimes. But they argued that his clinic and approach were an aberration. Moreover, they blamed Gosnell's crimes on the pro-life movement and the increased obstacles it placed in front of women seeking the procedure. "Kermit Gosnell is the result of anti-choice attacks on women," said one message distributed by NARAL on social media (Howley 2013).

Like the national controversy generated the year before by Representative Akin's comments on rape and abortion, the Gosnell murder trial generated debate that went far beyond the criminal fall of one physician. It raised some of the same issues, including issues of medical science, gender, partisanship, and whether there are moral distinctions to be drawn between "good" and "bad" abortions. But it raised additional concerns. At issue were inequality and racial prejudice, as Gosnell was widely reported to treat white women differently (and much better) than racial minorities. The role of the media and whether or not the majority of journalists and news outlets were taking sides in the abortion debate was also an issue. These were early echoes of what would become a national political obsession in the 2016 presidential race, with its swirl of fake news and accusations of media bias. Gosnell was convicted of first-degree murder in May 2013 after a trial lasting more than a month. He agreed to give up all appeals of his conviction and serve a life sentence in prison in exchange for not facing the death penalty.

These are just two, relatively minor, examples of the hundreds of times in recent years that the longstanding national debate over abortion has bubbled to the surface of public consciousness. Abortion has remained one of the most volatile and polarizing issues in the United States for more than four decades. Americans are more divided today than ever over abortion, and the debate colors the political, economic, and social dynamics of the country. In the first three months of 2017 alone, the *New York Times'* opinion pages included sixty-eight separate pieces that mentioned the abortion issue – an average of a piece every two out of three days. Abortion formed the main focus of fifteen of these articles, more than one a week. Every year, both the pro-life and pro-choice movements spend tens of millions of dollars and millions more volunteer hours engaged in the controversy. Perhaps most importantly, the terms that have come to describe the two sides of the debate, "pro-choice" and "pro-life," have become meaningful dimensions of cultural identity for many Americans.

As the Akin and Gosnell examples illustrate, however, controversy over abortion is always controversy about much more than just abortion. By debating abortion, people also debate questions of race, gender, sexuality, morality, partisanship, medical science, crime, and the media. Such issues are not raised alongside the abortion issue; they are *a part* of the abortion issue. Abortion has come to have layered meanings that touch on all these questions, as well as additional ones about religion, immigration, commercialization, and the role of government in the lives of everyday Americans.

The central argument of this book follows from such observations: the abortion debate is, and always has been, defined by the changing connections between the issue and other social and cultural divides in the American social fabric. From changing attitudes toward women, racial minorities, religion, and government, to technological and medical advancements, the development of the abortion controversy is embedded in the many other layers of conflict and change in society. The abortion debate is, in the end, a surprisingly empty vessel into which movements, politicians, and regular Americans have poured their anxieties and concerns. This book explores the (very long) history of the abortion debate in the United States. It shows how the pro-life and pro-choice movements were formed, how the issue has evolved, and the impact of the battle over abortion on politics and society. In doing so, it reveals the many ways abortion has been defined and redefined to meet the interests and concerns of different constituencies.

## How This Book is Different

The books written about abortion over the last several decades would fill most library shelves many times over. But many of

Introduction

them are not *about* the abortion debate as much as they are a *part* of that debate. They are written from the perspective of one side or the other, often by people who are themselves activists in the pro-life or pro-choice movements. They often offer both information and insight about the controversy. But ultimately their goal is to persuade readers of either the rightness or wrongness of abortion, with the history, facts, and analyses of their volumes filtered by that larger goal. A classic example written by passionate pro-life activists is *Why Not Love Them Both?* (Willke and Willke 1997), a book that first appeared in the late 1960s and went through a series of editions and name changes over the more than thirty years it was in print. A more recent example by pro-choice activists is *Targets of Hatred: Anti-Abortion Terrorism* (Baird-Windle and Bader 2001). The perspectives of such books are evident in the titles themselves. Many others make their central goal less clear, but nonetheless focus primarily on mobilizing support for one side or the other. Unlike such books, this one does not take a side on abortion. It instead uses the language and tools of social science to explain the interplay of the pro-choice and pro-life movements in the development of the abortion debate.

A great deal of careful social science research avoids these kinds of biases. But scholars have blind spots of their own. A chief problem in the academic study of the abortion debate is that many social scientists treat "liberal" and "conservative" social movements differently. Scholars see them as caused by different forces and being subject to different dynamics. They are thus typically studied apart from one another, and far more attention is given to liberal movements than to conservative ones. In the case of the abortion debate, this means there are many excellent books on either the pro-choice movement or pro-life movement, but relatively few about both.

This book will question whether the pro-choice and pro-life movements fit so neatly into the categories of "liberal" and "conservative" and thus can be treated separately. The history of the abortion debate shows that the relationship of the two sides to American politics has varied over time. It also shows how movements on different sides of the political spectrum can be analyzed using the same conceptual tools. The pro-life and pro-choice movements have very different political goals and are composed of very different organizations, people, and sets of resources. But they are nonetheless subject to the same political, cultural, social, and organizational dynamics. This book addresses both sides of the abortion debate. It focuses on how both the pro-life and pro-choice movements, as well as the interaction between the two, have changed over time.

Abortion has been studied carefully by thousands of scholars, over many decades, and in fields ranging from embryology to philosophy, history to public policy, literature to economics, not to mention sociology, political science, and related fields. The amount of work available about abortion is, from the perspective of any given reader, essentially unlimited. Like any book, this one cannot possibly cover everything that is written. But it does touch on all these various areas, and citations in the text have been carefully chosen to steer the reader toward key texts and original research that will allow further exploration of abortion politics.

## The Terms of the Abortion Debate

Before delving into any substantive or sustained discussion of the battle over abortion, some of the key terms must be defined. Both movements have made the terminology surrounding abortion part of the controversy itself, and some terms are frequently misunderstood as a result. I will refer to the people, groups, and organized efforts to reduce, restrict, or end legalized abortion procedures as the "pro-life movement," and the equivalent efforts to protect or expand access to legalized abortion as the "pro-choice movement." These names emerged in the 1970s, when the controversy over abortion became a widespread public issue. Prior to that time, the pro-choice movement was first called the abortion movement, and later the abortion rights movement (Staggenborg 1994: 188). The pro-life movement was known first as the right-to-life movement, and later the anti-abortion movement.

In using the terms pro-life and pro-choice, I make no claims that such labels accurately describe the movements or their goals. The pro-life movement rejects the idea that their opponents are providing "choices" and insist on calling them pro-abortion or even pro-death. The pro-choice movement rejects the idea that their opponents care about the "life" of women, referring to them instead as anti-abortion or sometimes anti-woman. Consistent with standards in social science research, particularly in research on social movements, I choose to let people decide for themselves what they should be called, rather than letting outsiders or opponents choose their name for them. As a result, I will use the same terms the movements use to refer to themselves: "pro-life" and "pro-choice."

The term abortion itself is also subject to controversy and misunderstanding. One of the difficulties in understanding the abortion debate is the fact that what people mean by the term "abortion" has changed over time. What we refer to as abortion today was called an abortion in much of American history only if it happened late in a pregnancy, as the next chapter will recount in more detail. Even today, most discussions of abortion refer to the deliberate ending of a pregnancy. The term "abortion" itself, however, refers to *any* premature ending of a pregnancy, whether it is deliberate or not. Another term for a miscarriage is a "spontaneous abortion," and approximately 15 percent of all pregnancies end this way in the United States (Jones and Kost 2007: 192). The abortion debate is not about such spontaneous abortions, however. When the term abortion is used here, it refers to a medical procedure in which a pregnancy is deliberately terminated through mechanical or pharmaceutical means. When we talk about abortion today, what we really mean is what medical professionals call "induced abortion."

## Abortion Statistics

With these terms in mind, a useful starting point for understanding the politics of abortion is to look at some basic facts about the procedure. The federal government does not collect centralized data regarding abortion. As a result, statistics need to be assembled by painstakingly surveying each individual abortion provider nationwide, as well as gathering and collating data from the health departments in each of the fifty states. These different sources of information vary in their quality; not all abortion providers respond to surveys, and each state health department collects different information and reports the results in different ways. The need to sift through and collate all this information means that abortion statistics are often delayed by several years. This monumental task of data collection in the United States has fallen largely on the Guttmacher Institute and its team of professional researchers. The Guttmacher Institute is avowedly pro-choice in its orientation, but the statistics it provides are widely respected as the most accurate available (even if its inter-pretations and policy recommendations are contested).

According to the Guttmacher Institute, there were an estimated 926,200 abortions in the United States in 2014 (Jones and Jerman 2017). This translates into a rate of 14.6 abortions per 1,000 women aged 15 to 44. The abortion rate has been declining for decades in the US. The estimated rate was 16.3 in 1973, the year the US Supreme Court legalized abortion nationwide. The frequency of abortion increased dramatically over the next decade, peaking at 29.3 in 1981 (see Figure 1.1) (Jones and Kooistra 2011). It has declined steadily since that time, so that the 2014 abortion rate was the lowest ever recorded. Nonetheless, these rates mean that a large proportion of American women have direct experience with abortion; somewhere between 22 percent and 30 percent of women will have an abortion procedure at some point in their lifetime (Cowan et al. 2016; Jones and Kavanaugh 2011). More globally, the abortion rate is even more difficult to estimate. One of the best estimates puts the rate at 35 per 1,000 women aged 15 to 44 – or more than double that of the United States (Sedgh et al. 2016); though at least one pro-life organization argues that this global rate is greatly exaggerated by using estimates of abortions not included in official government statistics (Jacobson and Johnston 2017).

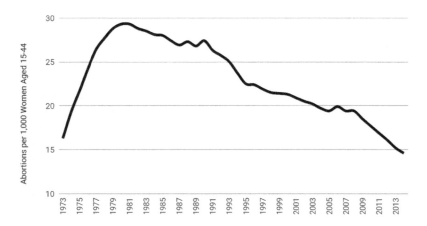

**Figure 1.1**   Abortion Rate in the United States, 1973–2014. Source: created with data from Jones and Kooistra (2011), Jones and Jerman (2017)

A significant amount of debate surrounding abortion focuses on when and how abortions are performed. Most abortions are performed early in a pregnancy, well over half (66%) in the first eight weeks and the vast majority (92%) within the first thirteen weeks. Only one percent of abortions are performed on women who have been pregnant for twenty weeks (five months) or more (Jatlaoui et al. 2016). Non-surgical medication abortions, performed by taking pills, make up an increasing share of the total number of abortions in the United States. The US Food and Drug Administration allows medication abortions in the first ten weeks of pregnancy. In 2014, 29 percent of abortions were conducted this way (Jones and Jerman 2017).

Abortion is relatively safe compared to other medical procedures. Between 1998 and 2010, there were 0.7 deaths per 100,000 abortions, though this rate varies greatly according to the point in the pregnancy when the abortion is performed. There were only 0.3 deaths per 100,000 abortions performed at eight weeks or less, but 6.7 per 100,000 for those performed at eighteen weeks or more (Zane et al. 2015). As points of comparison, one study of appendectomies found 1,800 deaths per 100,000 procedures

(Margenthaler et al. 2003); a (Swedish) study of tonsillectomies found a death rate of approximately two per 100,000 procedures (Østvoll et al. 2015).

Who receives abortion services is also often part of the discussions surrounding the issue. A common stereotype of those who seek an abortion is the teenaged girl who accidentally gets pregnant. Such cases do exist, but the majority of women (60%) seeking abortion are in their twenties, while less than four percent are seventeen years old or younger. The majority (59%) also have at least one child already when they receive their abortion. Approximately 14 percent are married and another 31 percent are living with a partner. Almost half (49%) are living below the federal poverty line (Jerman, Jones, and Onada 2016). These numbers show some broad patterns, but they also suggest there really is no "typical" abortion patient. Abortions are performed on women in a wide range of ages, relationships, and social and economic circumstances.

Litanies of facts sometimes play an important role in the abortion debate. At other times, they are largely forgotten. Like so many issues that become subject to public moralizing and debate, the controversy is less over the facts and more over what those facts *mean*. This book explores those meanings, both across time and across different groups of individuals. It focuses on the two social movements that have been central players in the abortion debate, but it also pays close attention to the cultural and political backdrop against which the abortion debate plays out.

## *Looking Ahead*

The next two chapters focus on the pro-life and pro-choice movements themselves. Chapter 2 tells the early history of the abortion debate, from the beginning of the nineteenth century to the 1973 Supreme Court decisions that legalized abortion throughout the country. This historical context is important, because the social, economic, and legal forces that shaped discussions of abortion during the nineteenth and twentieth centuries continue to have a profound impact on the abortion debate today.

The meaning of abortion has changed dramatically since that time, but echoes of the past continue to affect today's debate. Many people are surprised to learn that abortion was neither illegal nor rare in early American history. It became criminalized only at the end of the nineteenth century, spearheaded by the first anti-abortion movement, led by doctors. The modern controversy originates in the 1950s, when the first movement to relax strict abortion laws emerged, led by groups of lawyers, politicians, physicians, and, later, women's rights groups. Abortion became an issue of widespread public debate beginning in the early 1960s, and accelerating rapidly after the 1973 Supreme Court decisions. The pro-life and pro-choice movements have both helped to create this controversy, but they are also themselves the product of changing interests in abortion over this long period of history.

Chapter 3 looks at how the two movements have developed and interacted since 1973. The modern pro-life movement's roots in the Catholic Church colored the way it approached the issue until at least the late 1980s. The modern pro-choice movement's roots in the larger women's movement continue to be critical to its fortunes today. Both movements, however, are more diverse and heterogenous than is commonly recognized. Chapter 3 explores the diversity of each movement. On the pro-life side, the movement consists of several different mutually supportive but largely distinct wings, including one devoted to legal challenges and political pressure, one devoted to street protest, and one to outreach among individual pregnant women. On the pro-choice side, the movement consists of a political and legal wing that mirrors its counterpart in the pro-life movement. There is also a wing devoted to making abortion services available to women by supporting clinics that provide abortion and the patients who seek them.

With the origins and dynamics of the two movements established, the next three chapters explore the politics of the abortion issue. Chapter 4 sets the stage for this discussion by introducing public attitudes that surround abortion. It begins with an overview of public opinion on the issue drawn from a variety of different surveys. It shows how virtually all Americans identify themselves as either pro-life or pro-choice, yet relatively few support the stated positions of either the pro-life or pro-choice movements. Instead, most of the general public hold conflicted views of abortion. They find abortion troubling, favor many restrictions on the procedure, but are wary or opposed to an outright ban. The chapter also documents the relative stability of abortion attitudes over time. The overall percentage of Americans who support abortion under various circumstances hasn't changed very much for almost two generations, despite the dramatic change in public attitudes toward a variety of other social issues over the same period.

Chapter 5 examines how abortion does and does not affect American politics. Many are surprised to learn that abortion is by and large not an issue over which most voters decide directly which way to vote. Instead, abortion is politically important because it affects cultural – and hence political – identities. The labels "pro-life" and "pro-choice" refer less today to a person's specific views about the abortion procedure and more to identifying different "types" of people. Abortion as a marker of cultural and political identity has come at a time when the issue has become closely tied to the political party system. Republicans are pro-life and Democrats are pro-choice. The abortion debate has been a key factor in making both parties more ideological over the last several decades.

The discussion of the abortion debate through Chapter 5 focuses almost exclusively on the United States. Chapter 6 expands this view by comparing the American experience with the abortion issue elsewhere in the world. Controversy has surrounded abortion in most industrialized democracies. But it has been stronger in the United States, lasted longer, and reached into many more aspects of the country's political and social culture than elsewhere. This chapter explains the institutional, ideological, and historical reasons for this difference. The United States is different because of differences in its political system, and its longstanding and robust history of moral politics. And abortion has remained more controversial because its meaning has adapted to the changing anxieties and concerns of the public in ways that did not occur elsewhere.

Chapter 7 integrates the various parts of the abortion debate discussed in the previous chapters. The emphasis is on the interaction between the abortion controversy and other key divisions in society – particularly race, class, and partisanship, as well as the dynamics of other moral issues, including birth control, gay marriage, and capital punishment. In doing so, it underscores the nuances and changing meaning of abortion both over time and across different groups. These dynamic interactions are evaluated with an eye toward the future of the abortion debate. Understanding abortion politics is not simple. But understanding this complex issue provides key insights into the nature of how individual beliefs, social structures, and social movement outcomes are bound together.

# 2

---

# *The Making of the Abortion Controversy*

The status of abortion has changed dramatically over the course of American history. Not only has its legal status changed, but also its medical status, its moral status, and even the very meaning of the term itself. This chapter provides a short history of those changes, beginning in the early nineteenth century through the now famous Supreme Court decisions addressing abortion in 1973. This history challenges much of what people believe they know about the abortion issue. The history of abortion in the United States is not linear, progressing from centuries of rarity and condemnation to ubiquity and legalization. Instead, the legal status of abortion, along with its social implications, has fluctuated over time, influenced by social movements surrounding the issue and the changing structure of American society.

## *Abortion in Western History*

We use the term *abortion* today to refer to the deliberate ending of a pregnancy at any point between when an egg is fertilized by a sperm and when a child is born. But this meaning of the term is relatively new, dating back only to the nineteenth century. For most of Western history, the word abortion referred only to the ending of pregnancies after the point when a woman could feel the movement of the fetus – typically four or five months after becoming pregnant. This point was known as the *quickening,* which comes from the original Old English word "quick," meaning "living" (Brown 1993: 2448). The *Oxford English Dictionary* defines the term quickening as "to spring to life."

Aristotle famously dated the presence of a human soul to forty days after conception for male children, ninety days for females (Riddle 1994: 21). There were no known laws against the practice of abortion in ancient Greece, and well-known Greek philosophers such as Plato and Aristotle openly discussed the benefits to society (Gorman 1998: 21–3). Abortion was widespread in the Roman Empire by the first century BC, and Roman law stated explicitly that a fetus was not a person (Luker 1984: 12). Such views from antiquity carried forward to the views of abortion held throughout much of Europe during the Middle Ages and the Renaissance. Various means of obtaining an abortion were widely known during this period of history, and included the use of plants and herbs such thyme, juniper, calamint, quinine, and bitter cucumber. Abortions were widely performed, and generally not the source of debate or controversy (Riddle 1994).

When concerns were raised about ending pregnancies after the quickening in ancient Greece, the Roman Empire, or Renaissance Europe, they focused on the impact of abortion on the prerogatives of fathers and the safety of women who had them, not on today's concern over the fetus or the moral status of the procedure. Questions of inheritance rights and the ability of men to make life and death choices over the women and children under their control led to some restrictions on abortions during the last months of pregnancy, when many of the abortion procedures known at the time were extremely dangerous to the women who endured them. Most abortions were attempted using poisonous drinks or suppositories made up of herbs and metals. The alternative was the use of mechanical instruments which, like most invasive surgery during these periods, were a last resort because of their high risk of infection and death. Because of the dangers of these procedures, many of them were discouraged or banned outright after the quickening.

Historical discussions of abortion from these periods refer only to what we today would call third trimester, or late-term, abortions. Prior to the quickening, deliberately ending a pregnancy was not seen as abortion but as part of everyday medical treatment for women whose menstruation was blocked. This understanding was shared by medical specialists, theologians, and philosophers alike. Abortion as we understand it was largely unregulated, and often widely practiced, during much of the history of the Western world. The basic idea that the "ensoulment" or "animation" of life occurs at some midpoint in a pregnancy, dating back to at least the ancient Greeks, continued in various forms right through to the nineteenth century, spanning the period of the Roman Empire, the Medieval period, the rise of Christianity, and the Renaissance. Although a number of Christian thinkers questioned this idea over the centuries, it was the consensus view of political and religious authorities, as well as regular people, for most of Western history. The idea is written into Christian theology in the distinction between the "formed" and "unformed" fetus, and was the basis of Catholic Canon law for hundreds of years.

## *Abortion in Early American History: Legal and Common*

The United States inherited this tradition, as it had been codified in English common law, which allowed the termination of pregnancy for any reason up until the quickening. Those responsible for an abortion after the quickening could be held liable for a crime, but the offense was not as serious as killing another human being and was not punished as harshly (Mohr 1979: 3–4). In practice, then, women living in eighteenth and early nineteenth-century America faced little legal or moral impediment to abortion until late in a pregnancy. Women held a great deal of power over decisions to abort under the circumstances of the day. It was, after all, only the woman herself who could judge when the quickening occurred, and so it was the woman who could ultimately decide whether or not ending a pregnancy constituted an abortion or not. Moreover, the vast majority of terminations during this period were conducted in the home, either by the woman herself or with the help of close female relatives. Physicians and hospitals seldom played a role. As a result, women had control over decisions about both the appropriate circumstances for and techniques of terminating a pregnancy.

Induced abortion was not illegal, rare, or particularly frowned upon in the early years of American history. In the legal realm, there were no laws concerning abortion anywhere in the United States in the eighteenth or early nineteenth centuries. And abortion was widely practiced. The best estimates suggest that approximately one out of every four pregnancies during this period was ended by an induced abortion (Luker 1984: 19–20), more than the approximately one in five today (Finer and Zolna 2016). Most abortions were performed in the home, using remedies or techniques that were widely available in medical guides and health manuals. For example, William Buchan published *Domestic Medicine* in 1769, which was widely popular for decades and offered a range of techniques for bringing about an abortion (Mohr 1979: 6). Midwives, physicians, and patent medicine salesmen all advertised products and services for abortions, including in such places as church newspapers (Luker 1984: 18–19).

This is not to say that abortion was discussed openly during this time. Instead, euphemisms were generally used. For example, saying a woman was "with cold" was commonly used as a euphemism for missing a period, and advertisements for abortifacients would offer a cure to such a problem. "Female irregularities" was another phrase frequently used. But these roundabout ways of addressing abortion did not reflect moral condemnation of abortion. They were consistent with what the Victorian sensibilities of the time required of all discussions of female anatomy and sexuality, a "politics of the mothers" (Stansell 2010) that valued propriety and responsibility for family life to be kept private. It was the fact that abortion touched on sex and reproduction that made it a sensitive topic, not a particular concern with abortion itself. This sensitivity was reinforced by the widespread belief, which continues to some extent to this day, that abortions were needed primarily by women having sex out of wedlock, including prostitutes. While abortion itself was not subject to moral condemnation, the behavior perceived to be leading up to it often was.

## *The Rise of Physicians and the Criminalization of Abortion*

It was against the backdrop of abortion being legal, commonly practiced, and widely accepted (if seldom discussed in polite company) that the first movement to restrict abortion emerged. It did not call itself or think of itself as a "pro-life" movement. Indeed, it did not really think of itself as a movement at all. Its origins were in the early 1800s, and the first law criminalizing abortion was passed in Connecticut in 1821 (Hull and Hoffer 2001: 20). The movement did not really take off, however, until the 1840s. By 1900, every single state in the country had a law restricting abortion. This sea-change in the country's approach to abortion is the result of a variety of factors, including growing immigration and the increasing role of women in public life. But the change was led by the first anti-abortion movement: physicians who made abortion an issue because of their medical knowledge, both as a way to demonstrate that knowledge to society, and in order to increase their own status and authority.

Physicians in nineteenth-century America were not the highly paid and well-trained professionals that they are today. Nor was medical knowledge nearly as well advanced. There were few rules governing who could practice medicine, and schools offering medical training were unregulated and often established for profit rather than to advance medical expertise or serve the community. As a result, medical schools proliferated, offering a medical degree to almost anyone who could pay a little money for tuition, with little concern for rigorous training or passing on much medical knowledge. In Europe, there had long been a guild system governing trades that required a high level of training, such as medicine. Guilds operated as monopolies to insure that anyone who made a living by a particular trade had the necessary skills and expertise to do so well. Such a system did not operate in nineteenth-century America. Instead, the free market reigned: anyone could hang out a shingle and claim themselves a doctor, governed only by their ability to convince others to pay them. Historian James Mohr concludes that "by the late 1820s physicians, with a good deal of justification, were viewed by many Americans as menaces to their society" (1979: 31). Nor were doctors the only practitioners of the healing arts at the time; faith healers, patent medicine salesmen, and others who claimed that they could provide medical help, all vied for customers. People turned to all of these options, depending on their situation, to help care for the sick and cure illnesses. They did not necessarily hold physicians in higher esteem than any of their competitors, and given the state of training many physicians received, there was not any reason to do so.

Medical knowledge was advancing rapidly, however. A growing body of medical expertise could greatly improve the quality of care given to the sick, if doctors could be properly educated and trained. Yet there was little incentive for any particular medical school to offer such expensive and time-consuming training because there would always be others willing to offer a medical degree more easily and cheaply. Doctors needed a way to differentiate themselves from others, but they could not do so as long as they had no control over medical training and licensing. Physicians, in essence, faced a classic chicken-and-egg problem. In order to improve medical care (as well as their own social and economic status), they needed the state to pass licensing laws that would restrict medical practice to only those who had passed rigorous training in qualified medical schools. But, in order to convince the state to do so, they needed to demonstrate that they had unique and specialized medical knowledge that would serve the public good and was worth government protection – something they could not do without licensing laws in place to allow improved training.

The conundrum led to the first social movement focusing on abortion in the US. Abortion offered a path out of this chicken-and-egg problem. Physicians had long been more opposed than the general public to abortion because of the understanding provided by their medical training. They knew that fetal development was an incremental process that took place throughout an entire pregnancy, and thus rejected the popular notion of the quickening as a sudden, magical moment when life begins. Their training also led them to abide by the Hippocratic oath, which had long prohibited abortion. The first few states to explicitly ban the procedure in the early nineteenth century did so largely at the behest of physicians (see Table 2.1 for specific dates). The bans came about from individual doctors working through personal relationships they held with judges, lawmakers, and other elites. The public took little notice of these new laws. In every case they were not passed on their own, but as simply one part of much larger changes to criminal statutes. The new abortion bans applied only to those abortions conducted after the quickening. And in any case, the new laws were largely unenforceable given that they required knowledge of intent that only a pregnant woman and the physician performing the procedure could know.

The addition of abortion to the criminal code of several states in the early nineteenth century went largely unnoticed by most Americans. The issue became a public one for the first time only when the number and visibility of abortions rose significantly several decades later. Health manuals, medical law journals, and several limited scientific studies all agreed that abortion rates were much higher in the 1840s, 1850s, and 1860s than they had been previously. While we do not have precise or reliable statistics on the actual number, all the evidence together suggests that the abortion rate was somewhere between 20 percent and 33 percent (Mohr 1979). That is, there was one abortion for somewhere between every three to five live births. There was no single cause of this increase, though it certainly was not the result of social movement mobilization to promote abortion. Demographic changes, access to land, industrialization, improved communications, and the changing role of women in society all played some role (Lahey 2014a; Mohr 1979).

**Table 2.1** Year of First Abortion Statute Adoption, by State

| | | | |
|---|---|---|---|
| New York | 1828 | Colorado | 1861 |
| Georgia | 1833 | Nevada | 1861 |
| Missouri | 1835 | Idaho | 1863 |
| Arkansas | 1838 | Montana | 1864 |
| Indiana | 1838 | Arizona | 1865 |
| Alabama | 1840 | Vermont | 1867 |
| Maine | 1840 | Florida | 1868 |
| Ohio | 1841 | Kansas | 1868 |
| Iowa | 1843 | Maryland | 1868 |
| Massachusetts | 1845 | Wyoming | 1869 |
| Oregon | 1845 | Nebraska | 1873 |
| Michigan | 1846 | Illinois | 1874 |
| Mississippi | 1848 | Utah | 1876 |
| New Hampshire | 1848 | North Carolina | 1881 |
| Virginia | 1848 | Delaware | 1883 |
| West Virginia | 1848 | South Carolina | 1883 |
| California | 1849 | Tennessee | 1883 |
| New Jersey | 1849 | Rhode Island | 1896 |
| Hawaii (Kingdom of) | 1850 | Alaska (District of) | 1899 |
| Minnesota | 1851 | New Mexico | 1907 |
| Washington | 1854 | Kentucky | 1910 |
| Wisconsin | 1858 | Oklahoma | 1910 |
| Texas | 1859 | Louisiana | 1914 |
| Connecticut | 1860 | South Dakota | 1929 |
| Pennsylvania | 1860 | North Dakota | 1943 |

Source: Neef, 1979.

Abortion services also became a large, and successful, commercial medical specialty during this time (Brodie 1994). Advertisements for both abortion services and medicines sold to induce abortions at home began appearing frequently in newspapers around the country. An example is an advertisement for "Dr J. Bradfield's Female Regulator" that appeared in the *Columbus Daily Enquirer* on April 21, 1870. It promised to "bring on the menses" – a euphemism for abortion – in the privacy of a woman's home, thus preserving her "pride and modesty" (see Figure 2.1). The press also raised the visibility of abortion further by giving news coverage about botched abortions and professional abortionists for the first time.

For example, a newspaper in South Carolina smugly noted the arrest of a well-known New York practitioner known as Madame Restell in 1841, after the death of one of her patients (see Figure 2.2).

The first anti-abortion movement coalesced during this time in an effort to combat the rise in abortion rates as well as their

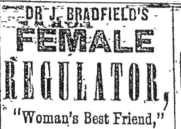

DR J. BRADFIELD'S
FEMALE
REGULATOR,

"Woman's Best Friend,"

Will bring on the MENSES when they have not been established, also when they have been suppressed from unnatural causes. WILL CURE RHEUMATISM and NEURALGIA of the Back and Womb. WILL CURE PAINFUL MENSTRUATION and RELIEVE THE HEAD, BACK and LOINS of those distressing pains and aches. Will check Menorhagia or "EXCESSIVE FLOW." Will cure "Whites" or Falling of the Womb, when it is the result of relaxation or bad health.

It is as sure a cure in all the above diseases as Quinine is in Chills and Fevers.

LADIES CAN CURE THEMSELVES of all the above diseases WITHOUT REVEALING THEIR COMPLAINTS to any person, which is always mortifying to their PRIDE and MODESTY.

It is recommended and used by the best physicians in their private pactice.

For a history of the above diseases, certificates of its wonderful cures and directions, the reader is referred to the wrapper around the bottle.

Sold by all Druggists. Price $1.50

Madame Restell, or Mrs. Lohman, a woman who has made a good deal of noise in New York, through advertisements in the penny papers, has been arrrested and is now in prison, on a charge of causing the death of a Mrs. Purday while endeavoring to procure abortion. She has doubtless amassed a fortune in two or three years by selling 'Preventive Powders' and otherwise professing to do indirectly what she is now charged with doing directly and criminally. Her race, we hope, is now run.

**Figures 2.1 (left) and 2.2 (right)**

continuing acceptability among most Americans. Physicians were at the forefront of this movement, as they had been at the beginning of the century. This time, however, they were far more organized. Horatio Storer, an obstetrician who had previously taught at Harvard University, helped to spearhead the crusade beginning in the 1850s (Olasky 1992). He enlisted the help of the American Medical Association (AMA), at that time a brand new organization (founded in 1847). This movement of doctors became increasingly vocal about the moral hazards of abortion. They argued that new medical science, which was not available to the general public, gave them unique insight into the origins of human life. Drawing on a line of philosophical and religious thought that had always existed, but had generally been a minority view, they argued that modern medical knowledge showed human life to begin at the moment of conception. Pregnant women, who may not have this knowledge, were thus putting themselves in grave moral danger by attempting to end pregnancies on their own. Only doctors, they argued, had the expertise and knowledge to know for sure if an abortion was acceptable.

The movement was remarkably successful at changing state laws based on this argument, particularly in the middle half of the 1800s. Abortion was one of the few things the majority of members of the young AMA could agree on during this period. A network of doctors, along with allies in state legislatures, coordinated with each other in both private lobbying and public calls for strengthening anti-abortion laws nationwide. In 1859 the AMA passed a resolution condemning abortion and calling for new laws to ban it (Luker 1984: 20). And state lawmakers heeded this call. By 1900, all but six states had passed legislation outlawing abortion, and states with existing laws strengthened their provisions (see Table 2.1). Unlike earlier in the century, several anti-abortion statutes were passed as free-standing legislation, not merely one part of a larger criminal code revision (the first in Iowa in 1858). Anti-abortion laws for the very first time began to hold the pregnant woman herself criminally liable for the abortion, rather than just the person performing it (the first such law appeared in New York in 1845).

## The Making of the Abortion Controversy

As noted previously, physicians held very different views about abortion than did the general public, owing to their knowledge that there was no sudden change in fetal development at the quickening, and the longstanding influence of the Hippocratic oath in medicine. The movement took its force, though, more from the social and economic concerns of physicians than from their moral concerns. State politicians, for their part, were often appalled at the crass commercialism of the growing abortion industry, as well as the dangers of poorly trained practitioners and harmful medicines being sold as abortion remedies.

This first anti-abortion movement was successful for a number of reasons. First, it was made up primarily of elites – physicians, and to a lesser extent lawyers and politicians – who had become active in the issue. Those who made up the movement had the resources, social and political connections, leadership skills, and other elements that make up any successful movement. Second, the movement faced very little opposition. There was no organized opposition to the changes the movement sought, making it relatively easy for them to influence state legislatures to pass the first abortion bans in the nation's history. Third, the movement's call against abortion was made salient to many state legislators by racial anxieties brought on by rising immigration to the United States during this period. An unprecedented number of immigrants came to the United States in the middle decades of the nineteenth century, most of them Catholic and not considered white by many native-born, Protestant citizens. Abortion was seen – not without some foundation – as primarily appealing to married, white, Protestant women, and, as such, might put the native-born population at a demographic disadvantage compared to newly arriving Catholic immigrants (Beisel and Kay 2004). As Horatio Storer, who led many physicians in opposing abortion, wrote in 1866, "... will the country ... be filled by our own children or by those of aliens? This is a question our women must answer; upon their loins depends the future destiny of the nation" (Storer 1866: 85). This concern dovetailed with a fourth factor in the success of the movement, the growing concern with the rise in women's rights and the desire by many male elites to erect a bulwark against the changing status of women as primarily concerned with childrearing and domestic affairs of the family.

## Abortion and Moral Judgment

The first movement to criminalize abortion led to significant changes in how abortion was understood and undertaken in the United States. Abortion became a moral issue, rather than just a medical one. Physicians, rather than women, became the most important abortion decision-makers. And access to abortion became more difficult for women who were not part of the elite or growing middle class.

As we have seen, abortion prior to the quickening (in today's parlance, abortion in the first two trimesters of pregnancy) was rarely considered to have moral implications before the nineteenth-century movement of physicians to change abortion law. What moral implications it might have had derived from the sexual norms that condemned pre-marital and extra-marital sex, thought to be its chief antecedents, not the act of abortion itself. Abortion was thought of in the same category of other topics related to sex, such as birth control. We are so steeped in the moral claims around abortion today that it is difficult for modern readers to imagine the possibility of the issue without its contemporary moral baggage, particularly in the United States. Consider it this way: few people today see different treatments of a urinary tract infection to have moral implications. It is a medical issue, one that can often be treated at home, though sometimes it requires the assistance of a medical expert such as a doctor or nurse. But the decisions surrounding it are practical, not moral. Most people once thought about abortion in this same way: a problem with menstruation that was often treated at home, and sometimes required the help of a physician. It was not a question of principle, or of good and bad. This did not change right away with the criminalization of abortion. The physicians of the first anti-abortion movement were frequently appalled by the easy acceptance of abortion by most Americans well after the laws banning the procedure had been established. But their movement and the laws they created did slowly change the country's understanding of the issue. The idea that there was something biologically or morally unique about the quickening faded away, replaced with the modern scientific understanding of embryology as an incremental and continuous process (Dubow 2010). But, most importantly, abortion became transformed from a practical (if perhaps immodest) subject to a moral one.

The way physicians presented the abortion issue in nineteenth-century America, as they made their case for being professionals in possession of new scientific knowledge, created an ideological contradiction that colors our discussion of the controversy even today (Luker 1984). On the one hand, they argued that new scientific discoveries had proven that human life begins at the moment an egg is fertilized by a sperm. Abortion was thus a moral issue, because it necessarily involved the taking of a human life. On the other hand, they argued that physicians should be the final arbiters of when and under what conditions an abortion might be appropriately performed. Both of these arguments were needed in order for the abortion issue to be used by physicians to accomplish their goal of improving their status in society and monopolizing control over medical care. Without the first argument, there was no need to look at existing abortion practices in a different way or give more weight to the scientific expertise of physicians than had traditionally been given. Without the second argument, there was no need to involve physicians in the decision-making process or call on their medical expertise in situations in which an abortion was desired.

But these two different arguments do not coexist easily. If one accepts the idea that a fetus is a person, a human life with the full moral worth of any other person, then why would physicians (who hold scientific expertise) be consulted rather than religious leaders (who hold moral expertise)? If one accepts the idea that physicians, with all their scientific expertise, should be the final arbiters of when and where an abortion should be appropriate, then the moral status of a fetus is dependent on those circumstances, and not absolutely set at the moment of conception.

One of the chief complexities in the abortion debate remains the difficulty of resolving these two different arguments. The contradiction also points out the importance of history in defining how we think about social issues. There is nothing inevitable or inherent in the abortion issue that leads us to discuss it in terms of the moral status of a fetus or the medical judgment of physicians. These issues are important because a movement of people – in this case, nineteenth-century doctors – made them important as a way to achieve a particular set of goals, goals that were distinct from the abortion issue itself. If a different set of issues had been raised concerning abortion during this period, or if it had never been made an issue as part of the professionalization of doctors, then the abortion controversy today might look much different, or it might not be a controversial issue at all.

# (Re-)Liberalizing Abortion Law

The status of abortion in the United States did not change very much after the first anti-abortion movement successfully criminalized abortion across the country. These laws did not end abortions. The procedure was still performed, but the locus of decision-making power over abortion shifted from individual pregnant women to that of increasingly professional physicians, who were, under the law, the final arbiters of whether an abortion was necessary or not in any given case. This status quo remained for almost three generations – from the late 1800s until the early 1950s. Abortion was discussed only furtively during this period, when journalists, authors, and others risked having their work censored if they raised it; some invariably did, and their ideas about the issue, including its connection to race, gender, eugenics, and the economy, were the starting point for the re-liberalizing of abortion law in the late twentieth century (Dubow 2010; Weingarten 2014).

By the end of World War II, scientific and medical advances over the previous fifty years had made it increasingly rare that doctors needed to perform abortion procedures in order to save the lives of pregnant women. At the same time, abortion procedures also became much safer for the same reasons. By the early 1960s, properly conducted abortions were medically safer for women than actual childbirth (Marley 1963). Physicians responded to these medical developments by increasingly performing abortions for the benefit of pregnant women's "health," rather than strictly to save their lives. In 1963 there were approximately 390 legal abortions reported in the United States; by 1968, there were 4,626 (Tietze 1970). Thus, while abortions became less and less necessary, they also became safer and physicians continued to perform them when they believed they were in the best interests of the health of their patients. Moreover, the definition of "health" broadened over this period, as doctors began to consider the psychological and emotional health of pregnant women in their decisions, in addition to their bodily health.

These changes in how abortion was being discussed and performed posed a problem for physicians, as well as for the hospitals they worked in: strictly speaking, they were breaking the law. The state laws passed in the late nineteenth and early twentieth centuries did not recognize the "health" of the mother as a legitimate reason for an abortion; the statutes empowered doctors to perform the procedure only when a pregnant woman's actual life was in danger. Physicians were, on the whole, comfortable with the changes in abortion practice. But they were uncomfortable with the growing gap between the legal statutes governing abortion and current abortion practice in which a broader definition of a woman's life was being considered.

The first step taken to address this issue was the establishment of hospital committees to review abortion procedures. Instead of individual physicians making decisions about abortion in consultation with their patients, groups of doctors and hospital administrators would make such decisions in order to comply with the law. Hospitals adopted such committees throughout the United States beginning as early as 1939 (Reagan 1998: 175), and, by the 1950s, virtually all American hospitals had one. Abortion committees had the effect of reducing the availability of abortions for most pregnant women, and abortion rates dropped substantially (Solinger 1993). Faced with having to justify such procedures to an impersonal body of colleagues and administrators, doctors were more conservative in recommending or agreeing to perform an abortion than they were when making such decisions with only their patients, with whom they often had a longstanding relationship.

Abortion committees reduced the number of abortions being performed, but they did not address the fundamental problem that doctors and hospitals faced: the laws surrounding abortion put on the books almost two generations earlier no longer reflected how abortion fit into the practice of medicine. This problem led to the second mobilization around the abortion issue in American history. Like the first movement of the mid-1800s, this one was again led by physicians. But this second movement, beginning in the early 1950s, sought to undo some of what the first movement had accomplished. The goal was to liberalize abortion law to give physicians more discretion by expanding the range of legitimate reasons for performing one.

The movement to liberalize abortion law was not based entirely on moral principles. The primary motivations for reform advocates were not the rights of women or a principled commitment to freedom of "choice" (ideas which developed later). Like the first movement to change the legal status of abortion, this movement was rooted almost entirely in social elites. Physicians were the primary constituency for the movement, but it also included politicians and lawyers who were sympathetic to the predicament in which the law was putting doctors when caring for pregnant patients. The reformers saw the issue more in legal terms than in moral ones. They wanted to modernize the law, not create controversy. The primary goal of the movement was not to create a right to abortion for women, but to preserve a right of physicians to perform them.

Other goals complemented this one. The birth control movement and growing acceptance of contraception, along with the early tremors of the sexual revolution, led many professionals of the period, including doctors, to support abortion reform as a logical step in the same "progress." As abortion reform efforts gained steam, the beginnings of moral arguments around concerns about fetal abnormalities and unequal access to abortion played a role in mobilizing physicians on the issue. The legal interests of doctors thus dovetailed with their other concerns, which were brought on by technological development and changing attitudes toward sex and reproduction.

These proposals for reform did not encounter widespread resistance and met with a great deal of success, at least at first. As a result of their efforts, the American Law Institute (ALI) issued a "model" abortion law in 1959 that explicitly permitted abortion to preserve either the life of the mother, her psychological health, or in cases of known fetal defects or when a pregnancy was caused by rape or incest (Tribe 1992). Colorado became the first state to reform their abortion law along the lines of the ALI model in 1967. It was followed in the same year by California and North Carolina, and in the next three years by Arkansas, Delaware, Georgia, Kansas, Maryland, New Mexico, Oregon, South Carolina, and Virginia (Reagan 1998: 222). In 1970, four states – Hawaii, Alaska, Washington, and New York – went a step further and decriminalized abortion entirely (Tatalovich 1997: 28). These reforms were widely supported among elites, not only in medicine and politics, but also in religion. Outside of the Catholic Church, the majority of mainline, as well as a number of evangelical, Protestant denominations and organizations publicly added their support for abortion law liberalization, including the Episcopal Church, American Baptist Convention, United Presbyterian Church, United Methodist Church, the Southern Baptist Convention, and the National Council of Churches.

## The Making of a Public Issue

The 1960s marks the first time in American history when the abortion issue became a truly public issue. Up until then, abortion had gone from being entirely unregulated for the first century of the country's history, through being tightly regulated and controlled by physicians, to being made more widely available under the liberalized abortion laws of the 1960s. Some controversy surrounded each of these changes, to be sure, but the debate over abortion across each was limited almost exclusively to doctors, lawyers, and politicians – a very small segment of society. The legal and moral status of abortion was not an issue that most members of the general public held an opinion about. So why did this change? Three main factors moved the abortion debate from the halls of hospitals and state capitals into the public spotlight in the 1960s: the Catholic Church's public opposition to abortion, the increasing political importance of the women's rights movement, and the high-profile media attention given to the plight of a particular pregnant woman, Sherri Finkbine.

The Catholic Church has been a leading voice in opposition to abortion in the United States since the late nineteenth century, and virtually the only organized voice of opposition to the movement to liberalize abortion law that began in the 1950s. Catholic priests and bishops publicly denounced abortion during this period, and they expressed their opposition at legislative hearings around the country as abortion laws were liberalized. They linked abortion to their opposition to contraception, euthanasia, and the death penalty, all of which the Catholic Church taught violated the sanctity of human life (Yamane 2005). For many people, this was the first time they had heard an explicit argument against abortion procedures. The argument was, moreover strengthened by the fact that, by 1950, Catholics represented 25 percent of the American population (Gallup 2016b) and the longstanding historical prejudice against Catholics in the United States had receded significantly, at least outside the South. The Catholic Church thus represented a formidable, organized force by which abortion started to be discussed by ordinary Americans.

On the other side of the issue, the growing power of the women's liberation movement helped to make abortion a public issue in its vocal support for liberalizing abortion law. Also known as second wave feminism, the women's movement was growing in political relevance just as the liberalization of abortion law was being debated. In 1963, Betty Friedan, a key leader in the movement, published *The Feminine Mystique*, which went on to become a best-seller. Just two years later, the National Organization of Women (NOW), a central organization in the women's movement, was founded with Friedan as its president (Freeman 1973). This growing women's movement advocated the idea that the "personal is political" and abortion became one of several "personal" issues that they advocated as needing to be addressed politically (Young 2000). As the women's movement gained in visibility and stature, they brought the abortion issue to the attention of the public, tying the liberalization of abortion law explicitly to the more general question of equal rights for women (Garrow 1998; Kesselman 1998).

As the Catholic Church and the women's movement brought abortion to the public's attention, on opposite sides of the issue, the media spotlight that landed on one particular woman's experience with abortion also helped transform the debate into a public one. Sherri Finkbine was a married mother of four living in suburban Phoenix in 1962. She was pregnant with her fifth child when she learned that pills she had taken for morning sickness had a drug – thalidomide – that caused birth defects so severe that only about half the children born from mothers who had taken the drug survived. Her doctor strongly recommended an abortion. She agreed, and they scheduled the procedure for the following week. In the meantime, however, Mrs. Finkbine was concerned that other women might not know about the dangers of thalidomide. She reached out to a friend of hers, the editor of the *Arizona Republic*, Phoenix's main newspaper, to urge him to run a front-page article about the issue. The newspaper did so the very next day, and the resulting publicity made the hospital abortion committee where Finkbine's procedure was scheduled nervous. After the article about Finkbine appeared in the press, they wanted assurance from the courts that they would not be prosecuted for an illegal abortion, as, strictly speaking, Finkbine's life was not put in danger by her pregnancy. The state courts did not provide such assurance, though they also did not threaten to prosecute. The hospital cancelled her appointment and refused to provide her with an abortion. Unable to find a provider in the United States,

Finkbine and her husband eventually travelled to Sweden to obtain a legal abortion.

The Finkbine case, as it came to be known, became sensationalist headline news throughout the United States. The news coverage was a major factor in making abortion a public issue; something that ordinary Americans might know about and discuss. It was the first time that the issue was covered by the media outside the context of covering police raids on unsafe, amateur abortionists. Finkbine was a suburban mom, not an unwed teenager. As television host for a popular children's program at the time, "Romper Room," she was not the poor, helpless stereotype many Americans had begun to associate with abortion. A poll conducted immediately after the Finkbine case showed that a slight majority of Americans – 52 percent – believed that she had made the right decision to have an abortion (Gallup 1962). But whether people agreed or disagreed with her decision, the more important point is that they had an *opinion* about the issue. For the first time, the question of the legal and moral status of abortion extended beyond physicians, lawyers, and politicians. It was becoming part of a national conversation about sexuality, rights, and the law.

# Roe v. Wade

The 1973 Supreme Court decisions *Roe v. Wade*, along with a companion case, *Doe v. Bolton*, were a watershed in the history of the abortion debate in the United States. They came after years of previous litigation and Supreme Court decisions on other issues, particularly birth control. Groups focused principally on birth control issues up until this time, including Planned Parenthood, as well as legal groups such as the American Civil Liberties Union, interested in developing the legal right to privacy and other citizen rights, had been key in challenging existing laws restricting both birth control and abortion. This included, importantly, the *Griswold v. Connecticut Supreme Court* decision of 1965 that articulated, for the first time, a right to privacy that invalidated state bans on the use of contraception by married couples (Garrow 1998).

The *Roe v. Wade* case itself began in the fall of 1969 when Norma McCorvey, a poor, single, twenty-one-year-old woman, became pregnant with her third child (Witchel 1994). She sought an abortion, but was denied under the strict Texas law that permitted the procedure only for the purpose of saving the life of the mother. McCorvey sued to overturn the law on March 3, 1970, and was joined in the lawsuit by a married couple, Marsha and David King, who cited medical and personal reasons for not wanting to have children at the time. The state abortion law was defended in the case by Dallas County district attorney Henry Wade. On June 17, 1970, the federal district court hearing the case ruled unanimously that the Texas abortion law was unconstitutional. The case was appealed directly to the US Supreme Court, which heard arguments in the case in December 1971 and again in October 1972, and issued its decision on January 22, 1973.

These facts surrounding the *Roe v. Wade* case include the relevant names and dates, but they do not tell us much about why this court case arose where and when it did. In particular, they hide the important role of the growing women's movement in the origins of the case. From this perspective, the *Roe v. Wade* case began before Norma McCorvey became pregnant in 1969. McCorvey's lawyers in the case, Sarah Weddington and Linda Coffee, had actually sought McCorvey out, rather than the reverse. Weddington and Coffee were young, feminist lawyers who believed that challenging legal restrictions on abortion would help women achieve full equality under the law. Weddington had had an abortion herself while in law school, having to travel to Mexico to obtain one because of the Texas law banning the procedure. She joined a feminist consciousness raising group soon after graduating from law school, which distributed information about the availability of contraception and abortion to other women. Coffee was Weddington's classmate in law school and was a member of the National Organization of Women (NOW) and another movement organization known as the Women's Equity Action League (Hull and Hoffer 2001: 114). Together, the two attorneys were actively seeking out plaintiffs willing to sign on to test the constitutionality of the Texas law. Marsha King, one of the other plaintiffs, volunteered after hearing Coffee speak at a feminist group meeting in 1969. She was herself already involved in efforts to repeal the Texas abortion law. Norma McCorvey had not previously been involved in activism, but Weddington and Coffee found her through a physician who was. The *Roe v. Wade* case thus started not so much from the circumstances of one pregnant woman, but from a conscious campaign by lawyers in the emerging pro-choice movement to actively challenge the bans on abortion that had been put in place a century earlier.

The *Roe v. Wade* and *Doe v. Bolton* decisions handed down by the Court together invalidated the abortion statutes in all fifty states nationwide. While most people are more familiar with the name of the *Roe v. Wade* case, the two are in fact companion cases that can only be understood in conjunction with one another. The *Roe v. Wade* decision established a woman's right to abortion and prohibited any law restricting this right before the point a fetus is viable outside the womb (a changing and difficult to define standard that has played a role in the battles over abortion since that time). After fetal viability, the Court ruled, states may place restrictions on abortions in some cases, but still not those where the "life or health" of the mother might be endangered by continuing a pregnancy. The inclusion of the health standard is significant, because in the companion *Doe v. Bolton* decision that originally came out of a case in Georgia, the Court defined the "health" of a mother to include not only her physical well being, but also her psychological and emotional health. These 1973 Supreme Court decisions did much to define the terms in which the battle over abortion continues to be fought today.

## Lessons from History

This short history of the abortion debate in the United States offers a number of different lessons. Perhaps the most important is that there is nothing natural about how we think about the abortion issue or the role it plays in politics and society. That is, there is nothing inherent in the abortion procedure, nor is there any unchanging historical standard, that makes the current abortion debate inevitable or even predictable. Instead, abortion has been constructed as a controversial issue because of a variety of historical events, the decisions of various individuals, organizations, and social movements over the course of the country's history, and the ways in which social environments have changed over time.

The starting point for this lesson is a recognition that the conventional wisdom about abortion as always having been frowned upon and outlawed throughout Western history is wrong. Abortion was in fact widely practiced and discussed in Europe for centuries. There was a range of opinions about abortion among Christian theologians, and in any case the debates only concerned what we today would call mid- or late-term abortions; it was never seriously considered that ending pregnancies before the fourth or fifth month could be defined as abortion at all. The idea that human life "begins at conception" is a modern one, not an historical one.

Nor were abortions illegal during much of this time. Indeed, the United States did not have a single legal statute governing abortion until the middle of the nineteenth century. Before that time, abortion was legal, discussed in books and in advertisements, and widely practiced. Perhaps most importantly, abortion was considered a practical, medical issue; not a moral one. Most Americans in the early nineteenth century had an "opinion" about abortion in the same way that Americans today might have an "opinion" about open-heart surgery (Luker 1984). That is, they had no real opinion at all, and the procedure was not controversial in the way it is today. Abortion was certainly not discussed openly, but this was due to its connection to sexuality, not because abortion itself was subject to moral condemnation. Everything connected to sexuality was discussed euphemistically and circumspectly during this period. Abortion is not naturally controversial; it has been constructed that way.

Another important lesson from the history of abortion is the way in which the construction of the issue has been defined by different social forces through different periods of American history. The first movement to ban abortion in the United States was driven in no small part by changes in science and the economy, both of which led to a growing need for physicians to differentiate themselves from others who had traditionally offered medical advice and care. Their use of abortion to make this differentiation resonated with a broader public, in large part because a period of rapid immigration had made many Americans concerned about the falling birthrate among white, Protestant women. As in the United States today, fear of foreigners was a significant political and social force. Half a century later, changes in science, coupled with a growing concern with gender equality, led to the liberalization of abortion law. Once again, the abortion issue reflected changes in American society, and was used by specific groups of people in order to achieve their particular goals.

Finally, history shows us that until the 1973 *Roe v. Wade* and *Doe v. Bolton* decisions by the US Supreme Court, the movements surrounding abortion were elite movements. Some physicians, lawyers, and politicians took notice of the issue and advocated for either stability or change in how abortion was addressed. But ordinary Americans were not involved to any great degree. This began to change in the late 1960s. And it changed dramatically and permanently in 1973 after the Supreme Court upended every abortion law in the country.

# 3

## *The Dynamics of the Pro-Choice and Pro-Life Movements*

The previous chapter demonstrated how the seeds were sown for the modern battle over abortion. The 1973 *Roe v. Wade* and *Doe v. Bolton* Supreme Court decisions led to dramatic growth of the conflict over the next several decades. The story of the abortion debate since 1973 is often told as a war between two opposing camps: the pro-life movement, which seeks to eliminate legal access to abortion, and the pro-choice movement, which seeks to increase access. Both the public and the movements themselves read the history of the abortion issue as a series of victories or defeats for each side.

The reality, however, is both more complicated and more interesting. Neither movement is a single, unified entity; rather, each consists of different threads, or streams, that co-exist uneasily and seldom flow together. The development of abortion politics since 1973 is as much a story about how the streams within each movement have meandered, and sometimes merged, as it is a story of the two movements battling one another. This chapter tells the story of the pro-life and pro-choice movements, and in doing so shows how the debate over abortion has evolved since 1973. As in previous periods of history, the ebb and flow of both movements are tied closely to the social, economic, and political changes that have taken place in the country over the last half century.

## Gathering Steam: The Catholic Church and the Origins of the Pro-Life Movement

The Catholic Church was the only organized voice of opposition to the movement to liberalize abortion laws in the late 1950s and 1960s (Jaffe, Lindheim, and Lee 1981). When the 1973 Supreme Court decisions were handed down, the Church's National Council of Bishops had the only pro-life spokesman, who journalists approached for comment (MacKenzie 1973; Van Gelder 1973). The official teachings of the Church, known as Canon law, have prohibited abortion since 1398. Ever since, the official position of the Church has been that any woman who has an abortion is automatically excommunicated, and any other person who assists her may be excommunicated as well (Jacoby 1998) (though Pope Francis issued a moratorium on the practice in 2015). As discussed in the previous chapter, this position has not meant the same thing through much of history as it does today; the meaning of "abortion" came to be applied to all deliberately terminated pregnancies only in the latter half of the nineteenth century. Before that, abortion referred only to those pregnancies deliberately terminated after the quickening.

The Church was able to draw on this longstanding historical record in arguing that opposition to abortion was "natural" and "timeless." It had not had a long track record of involvement in legal or medical issues in the United States during the earlier periods. Catholicism has been the faith of immigrants and foreigners through much of American history, and it has faced suspicion, prejudice, and a great deal of overt hostility by the native-born (white, Protestant) majority in many times and places. This began to change in the latter half of the twentieth century, since Catholics comprised approximately 25 percent of the US population in 1950 (Gallup 2016b) and anti-Catholic prejudice began to wane. The election of John F. Kennedy, a Catholic, as President in 1960 was a watershed event that signaled a growing acceptance of Catholics that was in many ways no less momentous than the election of Barack Obama in 2008 as America's first African-American President.

The Church used its growing numbers and acceptance to become increasingly involved in social and political issues it believed were central to its teachings (Byrnes 1993). In particular, the Church opposed the rapidly accelerating changes in attitudes toward sexuality and the family that took place during the 1950s and 1960s. For example, the number of young women who approved of premarital sex was approximately 10 percent in 1955, but almost 70 percent by 1970 (Wells and Twenge 2005). The number of divorces increased during this time as well, going from 2.3 per 1,000 people to 3.5 per 1,000 during the same period (Olson 2015) – a 52 percent jump.

The Church threw its weight behind efforts to slow or stop such trends. For example, it was a staunch supporter of Connecticut's ban on contraception, still in effect in the early 1960s. Not even married couples were allowed to use birth control in the state. When reformers attempted to open clinics that offered birth control to married women, the Catholic Diocese of Hartford used its influence to have the leaders of the clinic – Planned Parenthood's Estelle Griswold and Yale University physician Dr. C Lee Buxton – arrested and convicted of breaking a law that had been on the books since 1879 (Garrow 1998). They appealed their convictions to the US Supreme Court, which held in its 1965 *Griswold v. Connecticut* decision that the state could not prohibit contraception or the dissemination of information about birth control to the public. This was an important precursor to the later Supreme Court decisions on abortion, because it established for the first time a right to privacy in the US Constitution – the legal basis for the later *Roe v. Wade* and *Doe v. Bolton* decisions. The Catholic Church lost this case, but it signaled its interest and ability to intervene publicly in political and legal controversies as well as its commitment to opposing changes in how Americans were coming to view women and sexuality. The Church was effectively responsible for kick-starting the modern pro-life movement.

It was well positioned to do so. With thousands of parishes in every community throughout the United States, the Catholic Church possessed an organizational infrastructure through which meetings could be held, information distributed, and leaders found to oppose first the liberalization of abortion laws, and then, after 1973, the full legalization of abortion. Ironically, some of the fervor with which these resources were used are rooted in disagreements within the Church itself. In the years leading up to the Supreme Court decisions, the Church had undergone a number of reforms aimed at modernizing Catholic teachings and practice. For only the third time in four hundred years, the Church convened a series of councils between 1962 and 1965 that made dramatic changes to Church practice, including relaxing dietary rules, making marriage annulments easier, and holding services in languages other than Latin. Such changes were controversial, and pitted different factions of the Church against one another (Wilde 2013). Many within the Catholic Church advocated for reforms in the Church's attitude toward women, including allowing female priests and lifting the ban on contraception and abortion. But in these areas the "traditionalists" won out. An official Church commission recommended in 1965 that the Church allow some forms of contraception. Pope Paul VI rejected this recommendation the following year and reaffirmed the Church's opposition to all artificial birth control (Dolan 2003: 249).

Internal Church conflicts focused the efforts of traditionalists who sought to stem the tide of reforms in both the Church and the wider society. Kerry Jacoby, who has written a history of the pro-life movement, notes that "the Church, as the *Roe* came down, was in a crisis of authority, leadership, and respect. The youth were leaving, the clergy were in rebellion, and few things seemed secure in the Catholic world" (Jacoby 1998: 36). Abortion offered those within the Church an issue that might help them reassert the role of traditional authority.

Efforts by the Catholic Church to create a nationally coordinated movement against abortion were amplified in 1967 when the National Conference of Catholic Bishops (NCCB), itself founded only a year earlier, established the Right to Life League. The league coordinated various Church efforts to oppose abortion reform laws in states across the country. The

Church had previously distributed anti-abortion information through its Family Life Bureau, but the new organization greatly expanded these efforts and the organizational infrastructure to support them. With an annual budget of $50,000 provided directly by the bishops, the Right to Life League published regular newsletters, held conferences, and helped organize opposition to abortion both nationally and in individual states. Grassroots mobilization took place alongside increasingly vocal opposition to abortion in Catholic publications such as *America*, *Commonweal*, and the *National Catholic Reporter*, as well as increasingly public opposition by Catholic intellectuals such as John Noonan, Robert Byrn, Charles Rice, and Dennis Horan (Karrer 2011).

These efforts produced the desired result; by one count, there were several hundred pro-life groups nationwide by 1972 (Potts, Diggory, and Peel 1977: 363). The Church's Right to Life League began to organize national conferences in 1970 to coordinate the efforts of pro-life activists across the country. After the 1973 Supreme Court decisions, the Church decided that the group could gain more popular support, and be more politically effective, if it were not directly affiliated with the Church. The group was therefore spun off as an independent organization and renamed the National Right to Life Committee (NRLC) in May 1973. In order to underscore the new, non-denominational basis of the group, they chose a non-Catholic as the new leader of the organization: Fred Mecklenburg, a Methodist (Haugeberg 2017).

## The NRLC and Early Pro-Life Victories

The National Right to Life Committee worked quickly to establish a national lobbying presence in Washington DC, as well as state-level affiliate organizations in every state across the country. Strong organizations in states like Minnesota, Massachusetts, and Ohio served as models that were replicated nationwide. Even after breaking ties with the Catholic Church, the NRLC was by far the largest, most well-known, most well-funded and impactful pro-life organization in the nation. Other national pro-life organizations, such as the National Youth Pro-Life Coalition, Americans United For Life, and Feminists for Life, emerged in the years leading up to 1973, but all were overshadowed by the NRLC in terms of its level of organization, fundraising, visibility, and impact.

According to the minutes of its first Executive Committee meeting in early May 1973, the NRLC was created to "promote respect for the worth and dignity of all human life, including the life of the unborn child from the moment of conception" (Karrer 2011: 554). To do so, they developed several organizational goals. The first was to create a social movement infrastructure that was simultaneously national in scope and rooted in grassroots organizations in the states. The second was to raise money in support of pro-life lobbying efforts, something they were not permitted to do prior to their formal separation from the Catholic Church. The NRLC also had two political goals. The first was to support new legislation that would again place restrictions on abortion, after all existing state laws had been invalidated by the *Roe v. Wade* and *Doe v. Bolton* decisions. The second was to help overturn those Supreme Court decisions altogether.

The NRLC was a self-consciously secular and single-issue organization. The group sought to sever its explicit ties to the Catholic Church by putting lawyers, doctors, and other professionals in key leadership positions, rather than religious leaders (Rohlinger 2015: 58–9). It also tried to draw in potential supporters from across the political spectrum by focusing exclusively on the abortion issue; it took no position on issues such as birth control, sex education, poverty, and so on. This approach had its origins in debates within the Catholic Family Life Bureau. The Family Life Bureau leader, Father James McHugh, believed the pro-life movement could only be successful if it were led by regular activists rather than clergy, and did not tie abortion to other social or moral issues (Williams 2016: 93). McHugh's perspective was carried over to the new NRLC.

The activity and visibility of the pro-life movement exploded after the 1973 Supreme Court decisions legalizing abortion nationwide. The movement enjoyed a massive influx of new activists in the wake of the decisions (Luker 1984). Besides building its grassroots organization, the NRLC became active in supporting new pro-life legislation. More than two hundred new bills regarding abortion were introduced in state legislatures in 1973 alone. Within two years, thirty-two states had passed a total of sixty-two different laws restricting abortion (Rubin 1987: 127).

But the NRLC's most remarkable success came at the national level with the passage of the Hyde Amendment in 1976, three years after the *Roe v. Wade* and *Doe v. Bolton* decisions. The Hyde Amendment changed federal Medicaid law to read that "None of the funds contained in this Act shall be used to perform abortions except where the life of the mother would be endangered if the fetus were carried to term" (Shimabukuro 2012: 9). Since abortion had been legalized in 1973, the federal government had paid for about one third of all abortions (over a quarter million in 1977). The Hyde Amendment cut this number overnight by more than 99 percent (Fried 1998: 213). The Hyde Amendment has been renewed by Congress every year since it was first passed, although the exceptions permitted have varied slightly from year to year. It has had a significant effect on the number of abortions performed in the United States over the last forty years, particularly among poor women (Blank, George, and London 1996; Cook et al. 1999).

It looked as though this string of successes might extend to the passage of a Constitutional Amendment banning abortion altogether. The NRLC made a Human Life Amendment (HLA), as it came to be called, a major priority in the 1970s. Its efforts were joined by other groups, such as the American Life League, as well as by continued lobbying and activism of the Catholic Church. The National Conference of Catholic Bishops established a new organization, the National Committee for a Human Life Amendment, in 1973 just months after the NRLC became an independent group. The following year they initiated an ambitious Pastoral Plan for Pro-Life Activities, which called for the creation of a special "Respect Life" office in each of the eighteen thousand parishes nationwide and made the passage of an HLA one of Respect Life's top priorities.

The first Human Life Amendment was formally introduced in Congress only a week after the 1973 Supreme Court decisions (Williams 2016: 213). Passing a Constitutional amendment was a chief goal of the pro-life movement during this time, and the rapidly growing pro-life organizations conducted extensive political lobbying and public outreach in support of different HLA proposals. In 1974, four Catholic cardinals testified before Congress in support of an HLA, an unprecedented step at the time (Williams 2016: 218). Congressional passage of such an amendment was a real possibility in the late 1970s and early 1980s. Congress held a total of twenty-three days of hearings on a possible HLA between 1974 and 1976. The US Senate also held thirty-nine different roll call votes on HLA proposals between 1977 and 1983 (Strickland and Whicker 1986: 44). One HLA proposal in the Senate lost by only a single vote in 1982. The passage of a Human Life Amendment has not been a politically viable focus of the movement since the early 1980s, but in this period it was the number one focus of pro-life activism, an effort which came very close to succeeding.

The movement found more success in the legislative arena than in the courtroom, but enjoyed several important legal victories too. In 1980, the Supreme Court upheld the constitutionality of the Hyde Amendment in *Harris v. McRae*, cementing a key victory of the pro-life movement in the years immediately following the legalization of abortion. In the 1989 case *Webster v. Reproductive Health Services*, the Supreme Court upheld the right of states to ban the use of public funds, public employees, and public hospitals for performing abortions. Three years later, in 1992, the *Casey v. Planned Parenthood* decision upheld the right of states to impose a variety of restrictions on access to abortion services, including mandatory waiting periods for women seeking them. None of these decisions completely overturned the 1973 *Roe v. Wade* and *Doe v. Bolton* decisions that legalized them, but they did give state elected officials substantially more authority to regulate, discourage, and limit it, which the majority of states, at the behest of the pro-life movement, took advantage of.

## *The Rise of Direct Action Against Abortion*

The National Right to Life Committee and its close allies, both inside and outside the Catholic Church, have always focused primarily on the legislative and legal realms. In other words, they have tried to end abortion in the United States by making it illegal or, barring that, as difficult to obtain and legally available in the narrowest possible range of circumstances. But as the movement faced obstacles to eliminating legalized abortion completely, it turned its focus on more direct pressure against medical clinics that provide abortion services to women. Pro-life activists increasingly began to pray, picket, and protest directly in front of clinics, which led to tension between activists and clinic staff and patients. Sometimes protesters would try to convince women entering the clinics to change their mind about an abortion, and carry their pregnancies to term. This convincing could take the form of trying to speak directly with women approaching the clinic. More commonly, however, it took the form of yelled slogans, warnings, or even insults at those entering and leaving. In other cases, pro-life activists would try to physically occupy a clinic or block clinic doors. Social movement scholars call these kinds of strategies direct action, as distinguished from legal or legislative approaches to meeting movement goals.

The pro-life movement had engaged in these kinds of direct action activities even before the 1973 Supreme Court decisions. A Catholic organization called the Sons of Thunder occupied clinics in both Dallas and Washington DC as early as 1970, leading to the arrest of protestors in both places. Most direct action against abortion providers in the 1970s and early 1980s, however, was less visible. Protests were generally small, often consisting of just a handful of people, and, in most cases, were not frequent.

In the mid-1980s, the nature of direct action protests began to change. Protests became larger, more frequent, and more confrontational. A national pro-life organization focused specifically on direct action, Operation Rescue, was officially founded in 1988, though it had emerged informally several years earlier (Ginsburg 1998b). Operation Rescue used the Civil Rights movement of the

1960s explicitly as its model. Through protests, sit-ins, occupations, and other tactics, activists hoped to stop abortion in two ways: by highlighting their moral worldview to the public through expressive, high-profile actions, and by making it difficult or impossible for abortion providers to operate effectively.

Direct action eventually turned violent. Between 1977 and 1999, there were forty different bombings of clinics performing abortions, three kidnappings, and sixteen killings of clinic staff and pro-choice supporters. Over eight hundred cases of vandalism and almost 34,000 arrests occurred at clinics during the same period (National Abortion Federation 2016). The rise in violent disruption was an important new chapter in the history of the battle over abortion in the United States. What had long been a battle between elites, fought primarily through the legislative and legal domains, was now being fought literally on the street.

The pro-choice movement mobilized in response to the increasing protests and disruption, bringing activists of its own to clinics to help keep protesters away as well as protect clinic patients and staff. Tensions rose between those facing off at the clinics. Shouting matches between the two sides were not uncommon, and sometimes these turned into physical altercations. As media coverage grew to report on such incidents, popular debate over abortion increased as well.

A number of factors are responsible for the rise of direct action against abortion. The first is frustration within the pro-life movement at the slowed pace of legislative victories against legalized abortion. In the years following the 1973 *Roe v. Wade* and *Doe v. Bolton* decisions, the pro-life movement succeeded in substantially rolling back its availability. The Hyde Amendment put abortion out of reach for millions of pregnant women who could not afford abortion services on their own. Dozens of states took heed of pro-life calls for new legislation, and established a wide variety of new restrictions and barriers to abortion, many of which were upheld by the courts. Yet one of the key goals of the movement – fully overturning the Supreme Court decisions legalizing abortion in the first place – appeared less and less likely. At the same time, the chances of Congress passing a Human

Life Amendment to the US Constitution, which seemed a real possibility in the 1970s and early 1980s, dimmed in the late 1980s. Many within the pro-life movement became frustrated with what they perceived as a lack of continuing progress in achieving movement goals through legislative and legal means. Such frustration led some to look for alternative strategies for affecting change, including direct action.

Another important factor was the rise of evangelical Protestantism in the United States, beginning in the 1950s and rapidly accelerating from the 1970s onward. The proportion of Americans who identified with evangelical Protestant churches rose by almost 22 percent between the early 1970s and the mid-1990s (Putnam and Campbell 2010). The growing number of evangelicals brought with them a much stronger commitment to carrying their religious faith explicitly into public arenas, including politics (Blanchard 1994; Williams 2012). They also were more likely to see issues in stark black-and-white terms than members of mainline churches. Over the course of the 1960s and 1970s, evangelicals built a vast organizational infrastructure of churches, schools, think tanks, media outlets, and businesses that made it possible for them to engage in coordinated, sustained, and effective political action (Diamond 1989, 2000). And they were increasingly drawn into politics, particularly after Democratic President Jimmy Carter, himself an evangelical, threatened in 1978 to revoke the tax exempt status of private schools because so many had been founded with the principal aim of avoiding racial integration. The issue galvanized many evangelicals, motivating them to enter politics as well as reconsider their traditional connection to the Democratic Party (Micklethwait and Wooldridge 2004: 83).

Remember that the pro-life movement had, for most of its history, remained primarily a Catholic social movement. The rise of direct action within the movement marked not only a shift in tactics, but also a shift in the composition of the movement. Operation Rescue and other organizations that had engaged in mass protest (and sometimes violence) were dominated by Protestant activists, particularly evangelical Protestants. As newcomers to the movement, Protestant evangelicals were able to find their place in this new form of activism, which focused more on mass mobilization in the streets and direct confrontation with the pro-choice movement. The growing frustration with the inability to overturn *Roe v. Wade* and *Doe v. Bolton,* coupled with an influx of politically energized evangelical Protestants, combined to produce a marked change in the main focus of pro-life activism during this period. Though legislative and legal efforts continued, much of the energy and initiative of the movement shifted to direct action. Protests in front of abortion clinics became the face of the pro-life movement for most Americans, as they made for dramatic media storylines and were thus well covered in both print and television news.

The pro-choice movement reacted to direct action tactics in a number of ways. Pro-choice organizations called on their activists to come to clinics to help physically defend them, their staff, and their patients. Clinic "escorts" would help keep pro-life activists from blocking doors or harassing those coming in and out. They also fought direct action in the courts, initiating a lawsuit in 1986 that led to a long and complicated legal battle (including multiple trips to the Supreme Court) that was not fully resolved until 2014. Through this legal fight, the pro-choice movement was able to establish the right to sue direct action leaders under a law originally created to help police fight organized crime, known as the RICO (Racketeer Influenced and Corrupt Organizations) Act. Their lobbying, along with growing violence against clinics, led Congress to pass the Freedom of Access to Clinic Entrances (FACE) Act in 1994, making it much more difficult for pro-life direct action to physically disrupt the operation of clinics. First-time offenders convicted of blocking a clinic entrance could be sentenced to a year in prison and a $100,000 fine under the new law. By the time this legislation was passed, however, the size and number of such direct action protests had already declined markedly.

Direct action brought a great deal of attention to the abortion issue. But it also led to violence, including the killing of two doctors and three clinic workers by pro-life movement extremists in March 1993 and December 1994. Some in the direct action stream saw violence as potentially helping the pro-life cause by putting pressure on both providers and pregnant women to abortion services (Doan 2007). Ultimately, however, the violence that grew out of the protest activity led to repression by both the courts and the Congress. It also tarnished the image of the pro-life movement in the eyes of many Americans, as the movement as a whole became associated with the protests and violence of those engaged in direct action (Wilder 2000: 83).

## Further Evolution: Crisis Pregnancy Centers

As the energy and focus on direct action declined, a third facet of the pro-life movement became increasingly important: crisis pregnancy centers. Crisis pregnancy centers (CPCs) are organizations established by the pro-life movement to seek out pregnant women who may be considering abortion and convince them to carry their pregnancies to term. These centers typically maintain a small office that advertises free pregnancy testing and other services in order to encourage pregnant women to visit. They can range from a room in the basement of a church, to a suite in an office park, to a full-fledged free-standing facility that offers a variety of charity programs and even medical care.

Like direct action, CPCs have a history that pre-dates the legalization of abortion in 1973. Birthright, a Catholic network of CPCs, was founded in 1968, and by the time of the *Roe v. Wade* and *Doe v. Bolton* decisions there were perhaps a few dozen CPCs nationwide. That number was a few hundred by 1980, but began expanding rapidly in the 1990s. By 2000, there were an estimated 2,500 crisis pregnancy centers in the United States (compared to fewer than 2,000 locations that provided abortions that same year).

Today there are an estimated 3,000 CPCs nationwide, which the movement now calls "pregnancy resource centers." They have grown rapidly, in part, as a response to the protest, disruption, and violence that characterized direct action against abortion. Pro-life leaders recognized the harm this form of activism was doing to the reputation of the movement and actively looked for alternatives.

At the same time, many pro-life activists themselves were critical of street protest and sought a different way to be involved in the movement. The vast majority of volunteer hours devoted to the pro-life movement today occurs in these thousands of CPCs. The organizations themselves coordinate through national and international federations such as Care-Net and Birthright. They spend millions of dollars on advertising online, on billboards, in student newspapers and other venues, and outreach programs in both private and public schools. In doing so, they have introduced many Americans to a very different side of the pro-life movement.

Crisis pregnancy centers also go to the core debate being fought between the pro-life and pro-choice movements because their explicit goal is to co-opt the "choice" argument made by the pro-choice movement. CPCs, pro-lifers argue, increase the range of choices pregnant women have. Women who do not have all the facts about pregnancy and abortion, they argue, are given those facts. Some CPCs offer housing assistance, food assistance, baby supplies, and other material support that they believe might allow a pregnant woman who is poor and considering abortion to choose to continue her pregnancy to term. Others interface with adoption agencies in order to provide further choices. This is not all CPCs do, of course. Many use high-pressure tactics to guilt, trick, or otherwise coerce women to carry their pregnancies to term. The use of misleading or outright false information is common in CPCs. But providing services such as counseling, food pantries, and adoption allow the pro-life movement to take the wind out of the sails of the pro-choice argument that all women should have a choice over what happens to their bodies. CPCs attempt to co-opt the idea of choice, and channel it toward the longstanding goals of the pro-life movement – to prevent abortion rather than promote its availability.

## *Defending* Roe v. Wade

The pro-choice movement has largely been a defensive counter-movement since the 1973 *Roe v. Wade* and *Doe v. Bolton* decisions legalizing abortion. Pro-choice organizations have fought to defend the abortion rights established by the Supreme Court against pro-life attempts to reduce, circumvent, or eliminate them. The pro-choice movement has also evolved over time, responding to cultural and tactical shifts in the abortion debate. The pro-choice movement has some of its roots in concerns over population control. One strain of the population control movement continued to buoy the pro-choice movement through the 1970s (Schoen 2005), until it was eclipsed by the women's movement. Remember that it was feminist lawyers who originally developed the cases that led to the 1973 Supreme Court decisions. Key movement constituencies of women, students, and clergy, all of whom gained their initial experience with activism in the Civil Rights movement of the 1960s, took up the cause of women's equality beginning in the 1970s (Staggenborg 1994: 148–9) As the successes of the pro-life movement mounted, the pro-choice movement then became increasingly focused on the abortion issue alone, rather than a larger array of issues related to women's rights. The history of the two most important organizations in the pro-choice movement, the National Organization of Women (NOW) and the National Abortion Rights Action League (NARAL) illustrate this evolution. NOW was organized in 1966 with 300 charter members to advocate for women's equality in the United States. Its chief focus was on economic issues: ensuring that women had access to careers traditionally dominated by men, as well as equal pay for women doing the same work as men (Staggenborg 1994: 20). It was a decentralized organization throughout the 1970s, with several national offices spread throughout the country. NOW faced divisive internal struggles for the leadership and direction of the organization in 1974 and 1975, struggles that were in part a result of the poor organization and communication channels of the group (Freeman 1975). NOW's divisions also reflected divisions within the larger women's movement. Race, in particular, became a sticking point in the organization. Despite the fact that a number of core NOW leaders had been African-American, the group had a poor reputation in the African-American community, which criticized the group's focus on the concerns and issues of (middle-class) white women (Ross 2000). NOW's broad focus and internal strife limited its effectiveness in countering pro-life movement gains in the immediate aftermath of the 1973 Supreme Court decisions (Mansbridge 1986).

A second key organization for defending legalized abortion was the National Abortion Rights Action League (NARAL). NARAL was originally founded in 1969 as the National Association for Repeal of Abortion Laws, but changed its name following the Supreme Court decisions in order to continue its advocacy work defending the newly established abortion rights. Unlike NOW, NARAL has always been a single-issue organization, focusing on abortion rather than women's rights more generally. It has always used the importance of women's equality as its primary defense of abortion rights, however. NARAL is in many ways the pro-choice equivalent of the pro-life movement's National Right to Life Committee (NRLC): a highly visible national group with a singular focus on the abortion issue. NARAL, however, has never dominated the pro-choice movement in the same way as the NRLC did the pro-life movement in the years after 1973. NARAL has also been involved in many aspects of pro-choice activism, beyond just the legislative and legal focus of the NRLC. NARAL has changed its name several times over the course of its history, but has always maintained the same acronym. It continues to be one of the most important organizations within the pro-choice movement.

The two other groups that have played a central role in defending abortion rights have been the Planned Parenthood Federation and the American Civil Liberties Union (ACLU). Neither engaged with the abortion issue prior to the Supreme Court decisions, but both have been crucial parts of the movement since that time. Planned Parenthood was founded by women's rights and birth control advocate Margaret Sanger in 1916. After 1973, it became one of the chief providers of abortion services in its clinics throughout the country. The organization has been a strong abortion rights advocate, but has never focused exclusively, or even primarily, on the abortion issue. Consistent with its origins, it provides an array of reproductive services to women and families, including testing and treatment of STDs, cancer screening, and contraception. The ACLU focuses primarily on individual rights in the legal and political realm. They have been involved in many of the important lawsuits involving questions of the rights of women to access abortion services. Though not originally part of the modern pro-choice movement, they have increasingly joined pro-choice activists and movement organizations to help defend and, in some cases, expand reproductive rights for women.

Although there has been a steady decline in the availability and legality of abortion since 1973, the pro-choice movement has celebrated a number of important victories. In 1983, the Supreme Court ruled in two different cases (*City of Akron v. Akron Center for Reproductive Health* and *Planned Parenthood v. Ashcroft*) against a number of new restrictions and limitations on abortion services, including parental notification laws that did not include a provision for exceptions and a requirement that second trimester abortions be performed in a hospital. These rulings affected very few actual abortions, but the cases were important because the Supreme Court used them to reaffirm the core legal right to abortion that had been established a decade earlier. The most significant pro-choice legal victory in a generation was the Court's 2016 *Whole Woman's Health v. Hellerstedt* decision. In it, the Supreme Court determined that states could not create arbitrary rules governing abortion procedures in the name of protecting women's health if there was no evidence that such rules actually improved women's health.

The decision invalidated several of what are known as Targeted Regulation of Abortion Providers (or TRAP) laws, which impose particular medical restrictions on abortion procedures that are not placed on any other medical procedure. Such laws emerged in the late 2000s as a particularly effective means of the pro-life movement to create obstacles to otherwise legal abortion procedures. Such laws make it more difficult to provide abortion services, make those services substantially more expensive, increase the licensing requirements for clinics, and place a variety of workplace burdens on abortion providers (Gerdts et al. 2016; Mercier, Buchbinder, and Bryant 2016). The Supreme Court's *Hellerstedt* decision put substantial limits on such TRAP laws, thus restricting a key pro-life legislative strategy.

Such legal victories have been predicated on political work by the pro-choice movement. Like their pro-life counterparts, groups like NARAL, NOW, and Planned Parenthood engage in active lobbying efforts at the state and federal levels to protect the core legal right to abortion established by the *Roe v. Wade* and *Doe v. Bolton* decisions. They also actively support pro-choice political candidates across the United States. They have found the most success in the states of California, Oregon, Washington, Montana, Massachusetts, and Hawaii, where protection of legal abortion rights are the strongest in the nation. But, like the pro-life movement, they are a well-organized and well-financed movement across the nation that continues to fight for the movement's key goals.

## Movement–Countermovement Dynamics

The battle over abortion since 1973 has been determined crucially by the interaction between the pro-life and pro-choice movements, which became fully formed and mobilized in the wake of the Supreme Court decisions (Meyer and Staggenborg 1996). The issue no longer remained a difference of opinion argued by elites in courtrooms and legislatures, but a public, social, and moral issue about which there has been tremendous publicity and public debate. During this time, the pro-choice movement has been largely reactive, responding to changes in the makeup and tactics of its opponents. Having succeeded in establishing the legal right to abortion in 1973, the pro-choice movement has developed since that time largely as a countermovement to defend against attempts by the pro-life movement to chip away or completely overturn those rights. Pro-choice activists have at times tried to act proactively to expand the availability of abortion, but they have been overwhelmingly on defensive against pro-life attacks (Staggenborg 1994: 72).

The movements have fueled each other in their victories over the last half century. Each side highlights the threat the other poses in order to expand its own resources, visibility, and energy (Rohlinger 2002). In the immediate aftermath of the *Roe v. Wade* and *Doe v. Bolton* decisions there was an avalanche of new legislation in many states attempting to establish new restrictions on abortion. The pro-choice movement responded by lobbying against such legislation in state capitals and challenging the legislation that passed in court. After the pro-life movement helped pass the Hyde Amendment, restricting access to abortion by poor women, the pro-choice movement responded with campaigns to increase the number of private clinics providing abortion services and expanding financial aid for such services. Similarly, when the Supreme Court upheld a variety of new state restrictions on abortion rights in 1989 and 1992, the pro-choice movement was re-energized and redoubled its efforts to influence political campaigns so that more pro-choice politicians would be elected and more pro-choice judges appointed to the courts.

This dynamic has worked in the opposite direction, too. The rise of direct action tactics against abortion providers led to a widespread public perception that the pro-life movement did not care about women, particularly women in difficult situations such as having an unplanned or unwanted pregnancy. The growth of the crisis pregnancy center strand of the movement was in no small part a reaction to this public opinion success of the pro-choice movement. Each time either the pro-life or pro-choice movement appears to have advanced its cause, through the passage of a new law, court victory, or success in a major publicity campaign, the other side uses that victory to raise money and mobilize its own activists and campaigns.

Another important dynamic within the abortion debate is each movement's changing relationship with its own extreme elements. The pro-life movement seeks to end all legal abortion, and most activists within the movement agree that abortion is wrong, even if the pregnancy is the result of rape or incest. The pro-choice movement seeks to provide safe and legal abortions to all pregnant women who seek them, whatever their reason for doing so. One of the chief challenges both movements face is that neither of these positions is widely accepted by the American public (an issue which is discussed in much more detail in the next chapter). The largest and most influential organizations in both the pro-life and pro-choice movements recognize this tension, and therefore often advocate for positions and policies that move the debate in their own direction, but do not accomplish the ultimate goal of either abortion for all, or abortion for none.

However, each side includes activists and organizations unwilling to make these compromises. This had a profound impact on the trajectory of abortion rights in the early 1980s, when pro-life forces were unable to agree on the wording of a Human Life Amendment to the Constitution, thereby squandering a very real chance at overturning *Roe v. Wade* and *Doe v. Bolton*. Similarly, the pro-choice goal of "free abortion on demand, without apology" alienates a significant segment of the public and sometimes makes it difficult for the pro-choice movement to achieve more modest goals such as legislation protecting clinic staff and patients from harassment, or taxpayer funding for some abortion services, or framing the issue differently to draw in new activists (Kimport 2016). Social movement scholars often talk about a "radical flank" effect (Haines 1988), which is the tendency of a movement's radical wing to make the mainstream movement appear more reasonable to the public and thus increase the likelihood of achieving more modest goals. In the case of the abortion debate, it appears the opposite is true too; the radical flanks of both the pro-choice and pro-life movements have at times hindered their ability to make progress toward their goals. The dynamics *within* each movement, then, can be just as important as the conflict *between* the two movements (Rohlinger 2015).

A third dynamic has been the course of public opinion. The ideologies and goals of both movements have developed in ways that both impact public opinion and are constrained by it. In the 1973 decisions, the Supreme Court accepted the basic idea of the pro-choice movement that women should have a "choice" over medical care involving their bodies. At the same time, the pro-life movement was able to maintain a widespread public consensus that abortion is a morally undesirable act and not simply another medical procedure. In her influential study of the rhetoric of the abortion debate, Condit (1994) calls this the "choice compromise" and shows how much of the dynamics of the abortion debate in the United States has been driven by this compromise. In more recent years, the pro-life focus on CPCs and their rhetoric of offering more "choices" seeks to challenge that compromise.

The relationship between the pro-life and pro-choice movements is not unusual. Scholars have long studied the relationship between social movements and countermovements that rise up to oppose them (Andrews 2002; Dillard 2013; Lo 1982). What sets the abortion debate apart is thus not this dynamic between the two movements, but the length of time over which it has occurred, the amount of change that has occurred on each side, and the level of impact it has had on American law and politics.

The dynamics of contention between the pro-life and pro-choice movements reflect the changing meaning of abortion over time. Both movements have reacted to and reflected changes in the most salient public concerns. As we saw in Chapter 2, the pro-choice movement embraced population control arguments in the 1950s and 1960s, when they were both bipartisan and popular. But they quickly moved away from those same arguments when they lost public favor. In the early days, the pro-life movement actively downplayed religious arguments. Then, beginning in the late 1980s, they were emphasized. In each of these cases, the movements reacted strategically to changing social conditions to put forth the most persuasive arguments possible for their ultimate goals.

But the movements have not just passively reflected social changes. They have also actively fashioned the meaning abortion has in politics and in the general population. Movements "frame" (Snow et al. 1986, 2014) issues in new and creative ways that can have an impact on how the issue is understood by the public. For the pro-choice movement, the idea of "choice" has become fundamental to the meaning abortion holds for many people. Indeed, it is so central as to be part of the name of the movement itself. The point has been a key one in the legislative and legal battles fought both before and after 1973. For the pro-life movement, issues of government funding and government regulation have been the raw materials of their legislative and legal efforts to chip away at the broad abortion rights established by the Supreme Court. This perspective, in turn, has colored the way many people understand the abortion issue more generally.

This chapter describes the ways in which the pro-life and pro-choice movements have interacted over time. With this background, the effects of pro-choice and pro-life mobilization on American public opinion, politics, and culture can be explored. It is these topics which are the focus of the next two chapters.

# 4

---

# *Public Attitudes and Beliefs about Abortion*

Most Americans consider themselves either pro-choice or pro-life. This is perhaps the single most telling fact underscoring the importance of the abortion issue in American social and political life. Abortion is an issue on which everyone has, and is *expected* to have, an opinion. The abortion debate thus involves the entire public and is not simply an argument between activists in the pro-choice and pro-life movements. Public opinion surveys show that well over 90 percent of Americans identify themselves as either pro-choice or pro-life (Gallup 2016a). This chapter explores public attitudes toward abortion by looking at what people believe about the issue, and what these beliefs mean in their lives. It also looks at where abortion beliefs come from, and how they have changed over time. And finally, it compares American beliefs about abortion with the beliefs of people from other places around the world.

## *Abortion Attitudes Among Activists*

Before looking at abortion beliefs in the general public, it is instructive to first understand the beliefs of activists – those individuals who are actively working for or against abortion rights. They have helped define the terms of the debate in many ways, through the campaigns, advertising, outreach, and actions of their movement organizations. They have thus had a strong influence on overall abortion attitudes.

The basic ideological premise of the pro-life movement is that a fully human life is created at the moment a sperm fertilizes an ovum (egg), which typically occurs between a few hours and a few days after sexual intercourse (Jones and Lopez 2014). The human life created at this moment of conception is morally equal to any other human life, and thus should be entitled to the same full legal protections that all other people have in society. From this premise follows a fairly simple position on abortion: ending a pregnancy through abortion is always wrong, no matter how the pregnancy began, how far along the pregnancy might be, what situation the pregnant mother might be in, or what potential medical problems the fetus might have.

Pro-life activists are strongly united on this position. They believe an abortion is wrong even if it is performed in the first few days or weeks of a pregnancy. They believe abortion is wrong even if the pregnancy is the result of a woman being raped or a victim of incest. As Wanda Franz, the longtime president of the National Right to Life Committee (NRLC) explains:

> [A]bortion is not a solution for women who become pregnant as a result of rape. Abortion itself puts women at risk for psychological problems. It does not contribute to their healing. Even worse, by encouraging these women to abort, we are inadvertently causing them to take on the mentality of the rapist. We are asking them to attack an innocent victim, which is exactly what the rapist did to them. (Franz 2013)

Pro-life activists also believe abortion is wrong when a pregnant woman is too poor to raise the child, is unable to provide adequate prenatal care, or when a pregnancy would require a woman to interrupt her education or career. The only circumstance in which some activists believe abortion might be acceptable is when continuing a pregnancy might lead to the death of the mother herself. Approximately one third of activists in the movement believe abortion is wrong even in this extreme situation. "If you understand that that is another life, even at the peril of your own life, you always try to do your absolute best to save that child, to save that other life," is the way one pro-life activist has expressed this point of view (Munson 2009: 101). Though pro-life activists differ a great deal in their understanding of why abortion is wrong and how it might be ended, they are unified in their belief that abortion is always wrong, even in very difficult circumstances.

The basic ideological premise of the pro-choice movement is that a woman's life is fully equal to a man's life, and that this equality can only be realized if women have the right to make their own decisions about medical care. They do not accept the pro-life premise that a fetus is a full human being, but believe instead that it is a part of a pregnant woman's body until birth. From this perspective follows a fairly simple position on abortion: ending a pregnancy through abortion should always be a medical decision left to a pregnant woman herself, no matter what factors she uses to make the decision or how far along her pregnancy might be.

Pro-choice activists are strongly united on this position. When asked about her views on abortion, Supreme Court Justice Ruth Bader Ginsburg stated at her 1993 Senate confirmation hearings that "it is essential to the woman's equality with man that she be the decisionmaker, that her choice be controlling. If you impose restraints that impede her choice, you are disadvantaging her because of her sex" (Bennard 2005). Pro-choice activists believe this right should extend to abortion choices made on the basis of other lifestyle priorities, such as furthering the education of the woman or the needs of her existing family. The only circumstance in which some activists believe restrictions might be acceptable is when a pregnancy is close to full-term, and the fetus could be delivered as a baby that survives outside the womb. The pro-choice movement's position on abortion is summed up by a slogan often used in pro-choice meetings, discussions, and rallies: abortion on demand, without apology.

The pro-life and pro-choice movements thus have diametrically opposed views on abortion. Each grounds their belief in a different moral concern, while rejecting the moral concern of the other side. The pro-life movement rejects the pro-choice focus on women's equality by arguing the right to life is more fundamental than the right to equality. The pro-choice movement rejects the pro-life focus on the rights of the fetus by arguing that a fetus does not represent a separate and fully formed human life, and therefore is not entitled to special moral (or legal) status. Activists in both movements do disagree among themselves, both passionately and sometimes divisively (as we shall see in later chapters). But such disagreements are generally focused on the strategies and tactics of their movements, not the ultimate ideological premise on which the movement is based. Though they might differ on matters of emphasis and focus, activists on both sides are remarkably unified among themselves in their fundamental understanding of the abortion issue.

## The "Mushy Middle": Surveys of American Abortion Beliefs

Activists in the pro-life and pro-choice movements have spent more than a half century fighting over these diametrically opposed views, and both have spent enormous fortunes in time and money trying to convince the general public of their perspective. Despite these efforts, the attitudes toward abortion held by most Americans fall somewhere in the middle of these two points of view. Surveys of abortion beliefs consistently show that a majority of Americans believe abortion should be legal in some, but not all, circumstances. For example, the General Social Survey, one of the most carefully collected surveys in the United States, shows that in 2016 only 43 percent of Americans agreed with the statement that "it should be possible for a pregnant woman to obtain a legal abortion if she wants it for any reason" (Smith et al. 2017). The majority of Americans thus disagree with the belief of most pro-choice activists. On the other hand, the same survey shows that 74 percent of Americans agreed that it should be "possible for a pregnant woman to obtain a legal abortion if she became pregnant as a result of rape." This perspective is at odds with the belief of pro-life movement activists that a fetus is a fully human life irrespective of the conditions under which it was conceived.

Other polls are also useful because they ask about abortion beliefs in slightly different ways. The well-known Gallup poll asked Americans if they "think abortion should be legal under any circumstances, legal only under certain circumstances, or illegal in all circumstances." In 2016, only 29 percent of Americans responded that it should be legal under any circumstances and only 19 percent responded that it should be illegal in all circumstances (Gallup 2016a). Far more (50%) responded that it should be legal only under certain circumstances. The Pew Research Center, another reliable source of survey data on abortion, asks the question slightly differently, giving respondents four choices rather than three (legal in all cases, legal in most cases, illegal in most cases, illegal in all cases). They found that 59 percent of Americans responded that it should be legal only under certain circumstances (Pew Research Center 2016).

Surveys also frequently ask people about their views of abortion in specific situations. Table 4.1 shows results from the 2016 General Social Survey. Americans show different levels of support for legal abortion in different circumstances. On the one hand, a strong majority (75%) support legal abortion when a pregnancy is the result of rape, or when the mother's life is seriously endangered (85%). On the other hand, a majority (54%) also oppose legal abortion when a pregnant woman seeks one because she cannot afford more children, or because she is unmarried (56%). Abortion activists on both sides have a name for the views of most Americans: the "mushy middle." The term reflects the fact that the attitudes of most Americans toward abortion tend to vary, are sometimes inconsistent and, most importantly, do not reflect those of movement activists themselves. Beyond the situations listed in Table 4.1, other factors that change people's attitudes toward abortion include the age of the pregnant woman, the number of children already in a family, the time in the pregnancy when the abortion is performed, how the procedure is paid for, and the level of disability or birth defect faced by a pregnancy carried to term.

This difference between activist beliefs and the beliefs of the general public is not unique to the abortion debate; it is common in many social movements. Movement activists tend to understand their issues in black-and-white terms. Those outside a movement, by contrast, tend to have more fluid views of issues, even if less informed, and they tend to see more shades of gray, even if that sometimes means their views are not internally consistent. Survey results consistently show that the attitude of most Americans toward abortion greatly depends on the context in which abortion is being discussed.

**Table 4.1**  Approval and Disapproval of Legal Abortion Under Different Circumstances, 2016

| Reason | Approve | Disapprove |
| --- | --- | --- |
| Woman's health seriously endangered | 85 | 11 |
| Pregnant as a result of rape | 75 | 21 |
| Strong chance of serious fetal defect | 72 | 24 |
| Married and wants no more children | 45 | 51 |
| Woman wants one for any reason | 44 | 51 |
| Cannot afford more children | 43 | 54 |
| Unmarried woman | 41 | 56 |

Source: created with data from Smith et al. 2017.

Survey results show that Americans generally provide qualified support for legal abortion. The issue is not painted with a single broad brush in the minds of most Americans as it is for pro-life and pro-choice activists. They take factors about a pregnant woman, her situation, and the situation of the fetus all into account when considering whether or not abortion should be legal. These fluid beliefs are in contrast to the black-and-white messages of both the pro-choice and pro-life movements.

# *Surveys Are Not the Only Way to Assess Abortion Beliefs*

Gauging public attitudes toward abortion can be tricky with surveys, which are complex and difficult to conduct rigorously and scientifically. How a question is worded in a survey, what responses are allowed, and even the order in which questions are asked can have a significant impact on the results. For example, in addition to asking people about their views on the legal status of abortion, Gallup also asks people to make moral judgments about the procedure. In 2016, 43 percent responded that they believe abortion is morally acceptable in general, and 47 percent responded it was morally wrong. On its face, this result suggests that far fewer people are in the "mushy middle" on the morality of abortion than on its legality; people took one side or the other. This conclusion is premature, however, because respondents to the question on the morality of abortion were not given the option of answering "it depends" – they had to raise it on their own (and 9% did so). This difference in answer choices makes the results difficult to compare with other questions in which respondents were offered middle choices. In fact, most opinion surveys overestimate the number of people who hold the most pro-life and pro-choice positions simply because of the way survey questions are written and asked (Cook, Jelen, and Wilcox 1993). American attitudes are thus likely to be even less consistent with activists in each movement than most surveys report.

The problem of wording is especially acute in the case of the abortion debate because activists on both sides have radically different ideas of what counts as a "fair" or "unbiased" question. Both the pro-life and pro-choice movements fund and conduct their own surveys. Often, they are not designed to scientifically determine public support for one position or another; rather, they try to create "proof" that the approach or attitude or belief of the movement is the one supported by most Americans. As a result, social media and the internet abound with misleading, and in some cases outright false, claims about public attitudes toward the issue based on such surveys. For example, in its own survey, a pro-life movement organization might ask whether respondents "agree that abortion, the murder of innocent human beings, should be outlawed" while a pro-choice group might ask whether respondents "agree that there are circumstances under which abortion should be legal, to protect the rights of the mother" (Utts and Heckard 2005). In each case, the question wording is designed to lead the respondent to one answer or the other by including the movement's argument in the question itself.

A recent example of this kind of controversy is a 2013 *Washington Post* survey that posed the following question: "Several states are considering or recently have passed legislation that makes it more difficult for abortion clinics to operate there. Overall is this something you support or oppose?" A pro-life commentator suggested that this question wording was biased, because it did not include the pro-life narrative for such laws, and suggested the question should have read: "Several states are considering or recently have passed legislation *increasing health and safety regulations and oversight* that might make it more difficult for abortion clinics to operate there. Overall is this something you support or oppose?" (Nolte 2013). Changing the wording would likely have changed the results of the survey to show that public attitudes were more supportive of the pro-life position on this issue, because it would have included the pro-life argument about such laws, but not the pro-choice argument, in the wording of the question. The choice of phrases like "human life" versus "fetus," inclusion of words like "life," "freedom," "murder," and "choice" can all have an impact on abortion survey responses. Evaluating survey results thus requires careful attention not just to the numbers themselves, but also to the wording of the questions, to who conducted and paid for the survey, and what interests they might have in producing a specific result.

Surveys are also only one of several ways by which to gauge the attitudes and beliefs of people. The news media and even some academic research present the results of surveys as if they are synonymous with public opinion; however, in reality they are simply one measure of that opinion, and an imperfect one.

Although surveys provide some insight into broad patterns in the attitudes people hold about the abortion issue, they do not tell the whole story. Direct observation of people discussing the issue in more natural settings such as homes, cafes, gas stations, churches, and bookstores, as well as in-depth interviews, can help to round out our picture of abortion beliefs held by the general public. These more qualitative studies reveal a much richer, more complex, and more interesting set of beliefs than simple survey and poll questions can uncover.

When individual activists tell their stories, through interviews or other means, the richer context in which they understand abortion is often brought to light. Many older pro-choice activists understand the abortion issue through the lens of protests and unrest of the 1960s in which they participated. Others have deeply personal experiences with illegal abortions and botched abortions prior to 1973, which makes access to safe, legal abortion services particularly meaningful to them. Younger pro-choice activists are more likely to understand the issue in terms of the conflicting demands and desires of work and family. Often such understandings are closely tied to feminism and the feminist movement, but this is not always the case (Joffe, Weitz, and Stacey 2004; Petchesky 1984). Pro-life activists show a similar range of understandings. Some look at abortion through the prism of deep religious faith, others through concerns with gender roles and sexuality, and still others in terms of civil and human rights. Activists in both camps also increasingly understand abortion in partisan, political terms, linked to other issues and larger political party loyalties.

Interviews with regular Americans indicate that their views about abortion are not substantially different from those of activists in terms of the concerns, arguments, and connections they make about abortion. What is different, however, is that public opinion about abortion is surprisingly un-thought-out. Many Americans will firmly state a point of view about abortion, whether it be a pro-life or pro-choice view. But they have difficulty discussing the issue in any depth beyond identification with either the pro-life or pro-choice label. They stumble when asked *why* they are pro-life or pro-choice, for example, or when asked what the difference is between the two points of view, or how the issue is related to other issues such as women's rights or euthanasia or healthcare. Many Americans are unsure of the legal status of abortion and have never thought about the implications new pro-life or pro-choice proposals would have on themselves, their families, or their communities. Take, for example, this exchange with a woman in Oklahoma City whom I interviewed a number of years ago. She considers herself pro-life, but is not an activist and not involved in the pro-life movement. When I asked her if she thought abortion should be illegal, she responded:

> Gosh I was just thinking about that. That would mean like any medical procedures would be illegal. If it was illegal they couldn't do it, right? As my father would say, he thinks that when it was made legal, that the respect for life in general, death penalty and things like that went down. And so I think that legalizing it, they did I guess throw out a lot of that back alley kind of stuff. But I don't think it's just, "Well, they're going to do it anyway, so let's just make it kind of safe." I don't think that's the answer either. But I don't know. That's a tough question. Because being so adamant about respecting life and not wanting those things to happen, would I want it to be illegal? Yes, I would want it to be illegal but also would want it to be like abolished? I would rather it not exist at all. It's kind of like dealing with the reality of it. You know what I mean? Because you want it to be illegal because you don't want it to happen. But it's going to happen, so I don't know. Yes and no. That's not a good answer. It's not a maybe, I would say yes. Yes. I don't know. [long pause] I would say yes. I really would. But that's just a hopeful part of me saying that if it's illegal, then it won't happen. But I don't know.

I've quoted her at length because her response perfectly illustrates the thinness of beliefs about abortion outside of the activists of each movement. Her answers show that she has not thought very much about even the core issues surrounding the abortion debate. She is thinking aloud for the first time as she responds, unable to articulate a clear opinion even about the legal status of abortion (which pro-life and pro-choice activists would agree is the most important defining difference between the pro-life and pro-choice labels). She identifies as pro-life; indeed, has agreed to an in-depth interview about her pro-life views. Yet she is clearly uninformed and unsure about even this basic distinction.

Research that includes interviews with people about their abortion beliefs complicates the simplistic picture of abortion attitudes painted by anonymous polls and surveys. Yes, the issue is a divisive one and yes, many people hold strong opinions. At the same time, these opinions are not necessarily rooted in a deep understanding of the abortion issue, nor are they opinions that most Americans dwell on or discuss at length with others. Americans *identify* overwhelmingly as either pro-life or pro-choice, but what these identifications mean requires further explanation.

## The Basis for Different Abortion Beliefs

Why do people hold different beliefs about abortion? That is, where do abortion beliefs come from? There are three basic explanations: the politics of gender, the politics of sexuality, and the politics of identity. From the perspective of the politics of gender, abortion beliefs are driven by deeply seated worldviews about the role and the value of men and women in society. The first worldview sees men and women as having different, if equally important, roles to play in a well-functioning society. Men serve as providers while women serve as nurturers. Significantly, women are viewed as critically different from men in their nurturing role because of their capacity (and responsibility) for childbearing and childrearing. The second worldview sees gender as unrelated to the roles people ought to play in the family and society in general. Men and women, from this perspective, are not just equal but should have the same opportunities and choices to make in their personal and professional lives.

Legal abortion threatens the first worldview as it strikes at the unique childrearing role of women. Abortion is part of a larger, destructive push to erase the natural and obvious differences between men and women. The status of traditional housewives, who do not work full-time outside the home and whose role in the family is defined by raising children and running the home, is particularly threatened by abortion. Making abortion acceptable and widely available devalues those things – pregnancy, childbirth, and childrearing – that form the core of their contribution to their families and to the community. People with this understanding of gender see legal abortion as dangerous and threatening, even if they do not seek abortion services for themselves. Those who "oppose abortion and seek to make it officially unavailable are declaring," concludes Luker, a key architect of this explanation, "... that women's reproductive roles should be given social primacy" (1984: 200).

By contrast, from the second worldview, legal abortion is essential to the ability of women to have equal opportunities with men. Unplanned or unwanted pregnancies prevent both men and women from freely choosing the paths they want to take in life. Because women are the only people who can become pregnant, access to abortion is particularly critical to their ability to enjoy full equality with men in choices about careers, education, family, and so forth. Moreover, criminalizing abortion has the effect of devaluing some choices women might make (for more education or a professional career, for example) and privileging other choices (such as marriage and childrearing). In this context, the choices women make are not truly free even if they do not seek abortion services for themselves. Feminist author Katha Pollitt expresses this point of view when she writes that "A man's home is his castle, but a woman's body has never been wholly her own. Historically, it's belonged to her nation, her community, her father, her family, her husband" (Pollitt 2014: 4). In other words, legal access to abortion is necessary for women to be free. The politics of gender perspective thus see the causes of abortion beliefs as flowing from one of two more fundamental worldviews about the role of men and women in society.

The politics of sexuality offer an alternate, if related, explanation. From this perspective, abortion beliefs are driven by larger views about the proper role of sexual attitudes and behavior in social life. On the one hand, sexuality, particularly female sexuality, is seen as something special (and dangerous) that needs to be carefully managed and controlled. Sexuality should be limited by marriage and parental authority, especially for girls. On the other hand, sexuality is viewed as a form of personal expression and experience that should not be constrained by old moral rules of traditional institutions such as the family and the Church. Moreover, the government should not be involved in regulating what people do in their bedrooms.

Abortion, in the first view of sexuality, disrupts the traditional and important constraints on unfettered sexual activity (again, particularly of women). The threat of pregnancy plays an important role in restraining people in their sexual behavior, as it ties sexual activity to the potential for significant responsibility for childrearing. "One of the things that prevented my generation from getting involved in sex was the fear of getting a girl pregnant, and now that's gone," one pro-life man in South Carolina told me. Pro-life organizations like the Family Research Council help reinforce this view by arguing abortion is tied to living out of wedlock and having multiple sex partners (Fagan and Talkington 2014). Abortion is wrong because it circumvents the natural relationship between sexuality and raising a family. In doing so, abortion cheapens the sexual bond between men and women.

In the second view of sexuality, abortion rights are necessary for a healthy sexuality that is free of implications for marriage and childrearing. According to this view, individuals should be able to explore their sexuality without it being tied to traditional institutions. Sexuality is a human trait that everyone should have the freedom to explore on their own terms. "Women these days understand that their sexual freedom, even if it causes them some amount of heartache, is necessary for their future success," is the way prominent journalist Hanna Rosin (2012) puts it. The threat of pregnancy resulting from sexual activity also falls disproportionately on women, so abortion is needed so that women can approach their own sexuality on equal terms with men. The politics of sexuality perspective thus sees the causes of abortion beliefs as flowing from one of two more fundamental understandings of, and attitudes toward, sex.

A third explanation for abortion attitudes is the politics of identity. From this perspective, beliefs about abortion do not reflect well-thought-out attitudes toward the procedure itself (or even specific attitudes toward gender or sexuality), but instead serve as a signal of the overall type of person one is. In other words, to say one is pro-life or pro-choice is not so much about the abortion issue itself as it is identification with a particular social group; the labels are flags that allow people to stake a claim to being part of a particular moral community.

To be pro-life is to identify with a community that puts stock in traditional notions of family, traditional values (where the meaning of "traditional" is well understood if not explicitly defined), and religion (Christianity in particular). Using the pro-life label represents a commitment to following the same rules of society that served previous generations. A young pro-life woman in Minneapolis put it this way: "I see myself more in married life, raising some kids hopefully. And hopefully being able to teach them some of those same values that I've admired so much in my parents and grandparents." This perspective understands the abortion issue in terms of a larger worldview; it signals identification with those in society who understand that there are clear standards of right and wrong. A recent study of conservative evangelical churches in the United States found that "respect for life" and "pro-life" are terms used to differentiate the community of "us" versus "them," even as the abortion issue itself is seldom discussed explicitly (Bean 2014). Pro-life beliefs, then, come from the lived experience of being part of a particular kind of community.

To be pro-choice is to put stock in the diversity of forms that families and relationships can take in society. It signals membership in a community that values the acceptance of other lifestyles and different ways of doing things. When people who are pro-choice insist that abortion is a "personal and private issue," they are arguing for acceptance of the choices of others even when you might disagree with them. As a widespread pro-choice bumper sticker puts it, "Don't like abortion? Don't have one." Pro-choice beliefs are thus at least in part rooted in identification with a community that does not judge the decisions of others or subscribe to only one standard of morality in society.

The politics of identity perspective explains the causes of abortion beliefs as flowing from a sense of belonging in one kind of community or another, rather than on the basis of any detailed understanding of the abortion issue itself. The way in which pro-life and pro-choice attitudes signal particular identities has also been increasingly tied to partisan political commitments in recent years. To say one is pro-life is a signal that one identifies with the Republican Party; to say one is pro-choice is to identify with the Democratic Party. This is a good example of how attitudes toward the abortion issue have come to serve as a banner for identification with a larger political community. The close, but changing, relationship between abortion beliefs and political partisanship is addressed in detail in the next chapter.

## Complications in Understanding Abortion Beliefs

Each of these explanations for public beliefs about abortion – the politics of gender, the politics of sexuality, and the politics of identity – helps us to understand the source of attitudes about abortion. But the picture they paint is incomplete. Two complicating factors make understanding abortion attitudes difficult, even with all three explanations. The first is the way in which each treats abortion beliefs as epiphenomenal (superficial), rather than as important in their own right. In other words, each explanation understands abortion beliefs as derivative from, or reducible to, some other set of ostensibly more important or fundamental beliefs (about gender, about sexuality, about personal identity). The second complication is the way in which each explanation overlooks how the pro-life and pro-choice movements themselves, through their interaction with each other and their many efforts to reach the public, have shaped abortion beliefs over time.

If the origin of abortion beliefs really can be traced back to other, more fundamental beliefs, then understanding abortion attitudes would be a relatively straightforward affair. However, it turns out that beliefs surrounding the abortion issue are often important to individuals in their own right, and are not reducible to more fundamental beliefs about other issues such as gender, sexuality, and identity. People frequently behave as if their understanding of abortion is not just a proxy for their beliefs about something else. I have spoken to many pro-life Americans who have changed their views about many other issues in order to make them more consistent with their opposition to abortion. Some have even converted to a new religious faith (Munson 2009). Many who hold pro-choice beliefs have lost friendships, changed political parties, and left churches that they and their family had attended for generations on account of the abortion issue. For at least some people, then, beliefs about abortion are not reducible to other, supposedly more important, beliefs or worldviews. Attitudes toward abortion can turn on just small differences in how people think about the scientific explanations of how and when life begins. They can also be traced to different experiences people have with pregnancy, family, children, and other aspects of their lives. The politics of gender, of sexuality, and of identity certainly help us partially to understand where abortion beliefs come from, but they do not provide a full explanation.

The active efforts of the pro-life and pro-choice movements to shape attitudes toward abortion provide a second complication. Their ideas and campaigns have an impact on how the general public understands the larger abortion issue. During the 1980s, the pro-choice movement emphasized the importance of legal abortion as a component of the "privacy" rights of pregnant women as well as the need to keep the government out of the private lives of individuals (Ferree et al. 2002; Saletan 1998). These arguments were chosen to resonate with the public and increase support for the pro-choice cause. It is hard to say how effective pro-choice advocates were in accomplishing this goal (see more on that below), but the particular arguments they used inflected the debate over abortion in important ways. Focusing on privacy and government intrusion left the door open for the pro-life movement to argue for a variety of new rules that made taking advantage of abortion services increasingly difficult for pregnant women. The prohibition against federal funding of abortion and new laws requiring parental consent for abortion both were made possible by these arguments. After all, these restrictions do not interfere with the concerns of privacy or government overreach. These rules now have significant public support; 55 percent of Americans say they support the federal ban on abortion funding (known as the Hyde Amendment) and 87 percent support parental consent laws (Moore 2016; Saad 2011). By contrast, if the pro-choice movement had adopted more feminist arguments and focused on abortion as a basic civil right, or the need for "equal choice" for women (Graber 1999), these types of restrictions might have been harder for the public to accept.

On the other side of the issue, the growth of the militant stream of the pro-life movement during the 1980s that picketed, protested, blockaded clinic entrances, and engaged in acts of violence against clinics and abortion providers, reduced public support for the wider movement. Framing abortion in terms of life versus death, and suggesting that legalized abortion was morally equivalent to the sins of slavery, or the Holocaust (as many pro-life activists did, particularly those involved in direct action), simply did not resonate with most people, even if it did help the movement generate emotional fervor among many of its own activists. By contrast, if the pro-life movement had eschewed such arguments and focused instead on the humanity of the fetus, as they have in other times and places, they might have avoided the loss of public support they experienced in the 1980s and 1990s.

Our understanding of the different sources of abortion attitudes remains necessarily limited. There are methodological limits, to be sure, to using surveys, interviews, and other techniques to understand beliefs. But the limits are also imposed by the nature of the abortion controversy itself. Abortion's multi-layered meaning, built up over time and across multiple phases of conflict between the pro-life and pro-choice movements, has created a complex web of connections between abortion and a wide variety of other aspects of social, cultural, moral, and political life. The sources of abortion attitudes are equally diverse and multifaceted. We can identify the range of origins for these attitudes, as this chapter has done, but can never specify a singular, definitive cause.

## Attitudes Over Time

As the last two chapters have shown, the abortion debate has changed dramatically over the last fifty years. The legal status of abortion has changed. Two large, well-funded social movements have developed on either side of the issue, each spending millions of dollars and millions of hours of volunteer time trying to change the status of abortion and the attitudes of the general public toward the issue. Hundreds of bills changing the status of abortion are considered by Congress and state legislatures every year. A long string of legal decisions has altered the political and legal landscape on which the abortion debate is fought. And, perhaps most importantly, the social landscape of the country has changed dramatically. When the first states liberalized their abortion laws beginning in the 1960s, Jim Crow laws still operated in the South, officially segregating racial minorities from whites in society. The majority of adult women did not work outside the home. And most American households were just beginning to buy their very first televisions. Society today looks very different from the way it did a half century ago.

One of the most remarkable facts about American attitudes toward abortion over this half century is how little they have changed, despite these enormous changes in the larger society. In 1975, the overall proportion of Americans who believe abortion should be illegal under all circumstances was 22 percent. More than forty years later, in 2016, the number was 19 percent (Gallup 2016a). Conversely, 21 percent of Americans believed in 1975 that abortion should be legal in all circumstances, and 29 percent do today. Overall support for the policy positions of the pro-life and pro-choice movements has changed by only a few percentage points over the course of almost two generations. Public attitudes over the full course of those years is shown in Figure 4.2. The results from more specific abortion-related questions, such as whether abortion should be permitted in cases of rape, show similar stability.

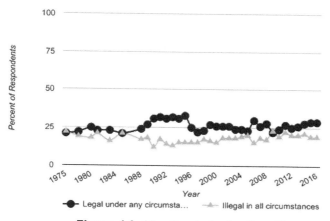

**Figure 4.1** Abortion Attitudes Over Time.
Source: created with data from Gallup 2016a.

American identification with the labels "pro-choice" and "pro-life" has varied a little more, but even here the change is modest. Twenty years ago, 56 percent of Americans considered themselves pro-choice and 37 percent pro-life. In 2015, the numbers were 49 percent and 44 percent (see Figure 4.2). The popularity of these labels shows more year-to-year fluidity because a significant number of Americans choose their answer based on political events happening at the time. The difference between the two has also narrowed, as the labels have become more closely identified with the political parties (the subject of the next chapter).

Why has there been so much stability in attitudes over time? One possible interpretation is that neither the pro-life nor the pro-choice movement has had much effect on public opinion, nor have the dramatic changes in society and politics over the last several decades. This is unlikely, not only because the movements are so well mobilized and the changes so great, but also because

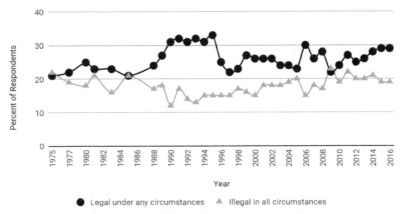

**Figure 4.2** Identification as Pro-Choice and Pro-Life.
Source: created with data from Gallup 2016a.

there is a lot of other available evidence that the meaning of abortion *has* changed over this period.

But then why do overall levels of support for each side in the battle seem so static? Another possibility is that the two movements have effectively cancelled out each other's efforts. This is no doubt true to some extent, though its overall effect on public opinion would be difficult to measure. The most likely cause, however, is simply that the stability of abortion attitudes reflects the way in which abortion maps onto different social divides over time. As different public issues connected to abortion have become less important or less controversial, they have not made abortion itself less controversial. Instead, abortion has simply taken on new connections to issues of public controversy. For example, population control is no longer a topic of much public debate, but the abortion issue has not remained closely connected to it (Ziegler 2009). The increasing public focus on healthcare issues has been matched by increasingly close connections, drawn by both sides, between medical care and abortion. In this way, the meaning of abortion has changed, and in some cases even the people who support each side have changed, but the underlying balance between the pro-life and pro-choice points of view has remained relatively constant.

## *American Exceptionalism*

The United States is not the only place with an abortion contro-versy, of course. How do the attitudes of Americans compare with those of people in other countries? Such comparisons are complicated by a lack of reliable survey data on the topic in many places. Surveys asking about abortion beliefs are far less common outside the United States. Moreover, the questions asked in such surveys are frequently different than those asked of Americans, and we have already seen what a significant impact the wording of the question itself can have on survey results.

One source of possible comparisons is the World Values Survey, which asks the same question of thousands of people in many different countries around the world. In the case of abortion, people were asked to rate, on a scale of 1–10, whether they think abortion "can always be justified, never be justified, or something in between" (World Values Survey Association 2016). Figure 4.3 shows the results from a number of different Western, industri-alized democratic countries. In the United States, more than 22 percent of survey respondents give the lowest score on the scale, saying abortion is never justifiable. This is more than in Spain (18%), Australia (16%), and the Netherlands (11%), and is more than five times more than in Sweden (4.7%). By contrast, less than 10 percent of Americans give the highest score on the scale, saying that abortion is always justifiable. Compare this number to 16 percent in Spain, 15 percent in Australia, 19 percent in the Netherlands, and 44 percent in Sweden. Overall, then, American abortion attitudes are exceptional compared to many European countries; the general population in the United States is consid-erably more pro-life than in these other places. Elsewhere around the world, however, particularly outside of industrialized democ-racies, public attitudes are more pro-life than even the United States. In Colombia, for example, 73 percent of those surveyed said abortion was never justifiable, as did 65 percent in Malaysia and 61 percent in Nigeria.

Beyond the comparison of survey results, the abortion debate in the United States is exceptional because of how visible it is,

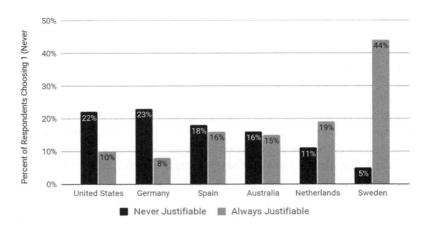

**Figure 4.3** Abortion Attitudes in Different Western Countries.
Source: created with data from World Values Survey 2016 (Wave 6, 2010–14)

how commonly issues of abortion arise in American culture, and how central the issue has become in American politics. Abortion is omnipresent in state legislatures around the country. A total of eighty-six new laws governing abortion passed at the state level in 2016 alone, thirty favored by the pro-choice movement and fifty-six favored by the pro-life movement (NARAL Pro-Choice America and Naral Pro-Choice America Foundation 2017). Abortion was a regular issue in the 2016 presidential campaign, as it has been in every presidential race in the United States for the last several decades. Thousands of billboards throughout the country are devoted to conveying pro-life or pro-choice messages to the American public. In short, no other country in the world matches the US in the level of contentiousness of the abortion debate. People have different opinions about the issue throughout the world, but the United States is unique in the centrality of the issue in public consciousness. The difference lies in the extent to which the pro-life and pro-choice movements continue to mobilize around the issue.

# *Conclusion*

The majority of Americans give qualified support for legal abortion under some circumstances, although their understandings of the issue are both diverse and complicated. This is the one-sentence summary of abortion attitudes in the United States. Most Americans do not support the view of abortion held by activists in either the pro-life or pro-choice movements. Unlike pro-life activists, the majority of Americans do not want to criminalize all abortion. Unlike pro-choice activists, most Americans do not want abortion to be legal for any reason at all stages of pregnancy. Instead, the majority of Americans are in the "mushy middle," where the issue of abortion is not clear cut, and their opinions about its moral and legal status depend heavily on the context in which a pregnancy, and an abortion, are being considered.

The abortion attitudes of Americans come from larger constellations of values and worldviews connected to gender, sexuality, and identity. In the last several decades, they have also come to be connected to political partisanship. Being pro-choice or pro-life thus is not related simply to a person's understanding and evaluation of the biology of human pregnancy. For most people, the issue is more than the question of whether life begins at conception (as the pro-life movement insists) or whether abortion is necessary for women's equality (as the pro-choice movement insists). Instead, attitudes are tied to a larger constellation of concerns and experiences in people's lives. They adopt the label of "pro-life" or "pro-choice" because of what they think it indicates about the type of person they are and the particular community of which they are a part.

These conclusions about abortion attitudes in the United States are generally true of abortion attitudes in many other Western, industrialized democracies. Public opinion is split on the issue in many places. But the United States differs in important ways, too. Attitudes are on the whole more pro-life and less pro-choice than in European countries. But most importantly, abortion is a highly visible, politically salient, ongoing social concern in the US. The pro-life and pro-choice movements continue to mobilize tens of thousands of activists and millions of dollars every year around this issue. Abortion is thus a topic of regular discussion in schools, on radio shows, billboards, and television broadcasts, at dinner parties, and in chats among friends. By contrast, the issue is rarely raised in any of these kinds of venues in European countries. People have different attitudes toward abortion in these places, but it is a settled issue. What makes abortion of such central importance in the United States? This question is taken up in the next chapter.

# 5

## The Impact of Abortion on American Politics

This chapter highlights the way in which the abortion issue does and does not influence American politics today. The debate over abortion is frequently visible in American political campaigns, but what role does it play in determining the outcome of elections? How does it fit into the political system among the other social and moral issues? And how do the pro-life and pro-choice movements impact the dynamics of American politics? The focus here is the contemporary United States, including the 2016 Presidential election, but answering these questions also requires an occasional look back at the historical events that created today's political dynamics. In a nutshell: abortion plays an extremely important role in American politics today, but one that is more complicated, and not nearly as direct, as most people assume.

### The Abortion Issue Seldom Decides Elections

Abortion figures prominently in many American election campaigns, from national contests all the way down to local elections. Candidates for elected office today are almost always known by the public to be either pro-choice or pro-life. They frequently debate each other and run advertisements about the issue (or the position of their opponent). In 2014, longtime US Senator from Colorado Mark Udall used his very first campaign advertisement to attack his opponent, Cory Gardner, for opposing abortion rights (Bartels 2014). Political commentators later noted that the entire Senate campaign in Colorado revolved around the abortion issue (Paulson 2014), which has happened elsewhere around the country at all levels of government.

For their part, pro-life and pro-choice organizations are active in these campaigns, funneling money and mobilizing their activists to support one candidate or another, even in very local races that have little impact on abortion rules or regulations. Planned Parenthood of Oregon, for example, offers formal endorsements and support for local school board candidates they have identified as pro-choice. In a recent city council race in Omaha, Nebraska, one candidate identified his anti-abortion activism as one of his key qualifications for office (Esch 2017). The media invariably includes the abortion issue in its coverage of political contests. On the surface, then, abortion appears to be a key issue that helps decide, or at least influence, election campaigns.

But the evidence suggests that abortion is not decisive when it comes to determining the outcome of elections. There are certainly single-issue voters who will vote for candidates based on their pro-choice/pro-life position, but their overall numbers in the population are small. In any case, such voters are roughly equally divided on each side of the abortion debate, meaning they effectively cancel each other out in electoral terms. For the vast majority of the public, abortion is simply not a key issue they consider when deciding their vote. Seldom do more than two percent of American voters list abortion as being the most important issue in an election.

The 2016 presidential race between Democrat Hillary Clinton and Republican Donald Trump exemplifies the role, or lack thereof, of the abortion issue within individual elections. Social media such as Facebook and Twitter were full of pro-life and pro-choice slogans and advertisements during the campaign, but neither candidate made it a central issue in their stump speeches, despite the fact that a vacancy on the Supreme Court was an important issue (and could have a direct impact on the legal status of abortion). Abortion was raised only once in the debates between the two candidates and voters did not report that abortion was particularly salient to their evaluation of the candidates. The Pew Research Center reported in July 2016 that 45 percent of voters viewed abortion as "very important" to their vote, but twelve out of thirteen other issues actually ranked as *more* important in the survey (Doherty, Kiley, and Johnson 2016) (see Figure 5.1). Only the treatment of gay, lesbian, and transgender people ranked lower. This is consistent with subsequent exit polls done on election night in 2016, which showed that abortion was not one of the top cited issues of concern to voters (foreign policy, immigration, the economy, and terrorism were the most frequently mentioned) (Huang et al. 2016). And although the 2016 presidential race was historically unique in many respects, it followed a well-known pattern with respect to abortion; was raised and used in the campaign, but voters ultimately did not use it to determine their votes. Since abortion became a public issue decades ago, it has seldom been considered one of the most important issues by voters when they enter the voting booth.

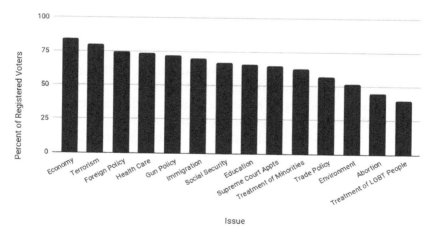

**Figure 5.1** Voters Who Say Issue Is "Very Important" to Their 2016 Vote.
Source: created with data from Doherty et al. 2016

Even if abortion were one of the top issues for voters, it still might not have a decisive impact on who wins any given election. A substantial body of research in political science has established that issues themselves are overrated as drivers of electoral outcomes. In his groundbreaking work, political scientist Philip Converse (1964) showed that most Americans do not have well-developed, internally consistent ideologies on which they base their votes. Instead, voters tend to be swayed by factors such as the current state of the economy, their own recent economic circumstances, and their association with political parties. Converse's work has become the conventional wisdom in political science since that time, with a wide range of subsequent studies confirming the basic insight that voters do not hold a stable set of consistent beliefs about non-economic issues, nor do their beliefs about non-economic issues drive their voting behavior (e.g. Kinder 1998, Fiorina et al. 2010). "It's the economy, stupid" was a catch-phrase of Bill Clinton's presidential campaigns in the 1990s, and research into voting behavior tends to support it: people vote with their pocketbooks, not on social issues.

## Abortion and Partisanship

Political pundits and journalists have become accustomed to talking about social issues in terms of a "culture war" in the United States, implying that Americans have coalesced into two mutually exclusive, hostile camps. Members of each camp are presumed to hold firm beliefs about a wide variety of issues that are the polar opposite of the beliefs held by the other camp (Hunter 1992, 1994). The data on public attitudes, however, simply do not bear this idea out. "The fairest reading of the evidence suggests that, across the issue spectrum, Americans are not as far apart as the pundits would have you believe," explains political scientist David Campbell (2006: 61). Looking across forty-eight different issues, DiMaggio and his colleagues have found that overall public opinion has actually moved closer together rather than farther apart over the last several decades (DiMaggio, Evans, and Bryson 1996; Evans, Bryson, and DiMaggio 2001). This and subsequent research (e.g. Fiorina et al. 2008) has shown that the country is not nearly as divided as the idea of a culture war suggests, but that there are two exceptions: abortion and party identification.

Abortion differs from most social issues in that public attitudes about it are more polarized than ever. This is one of the important ways in which abortion remains relevant, if not central, to American political dynamics. As the country has moved toward increasing consensus on issues ranging from women's equality to civil rights for minorities, from gun control to premarital sex, people have become increasingly divided about abortion, even if the *extent* of that polarization among ordinary Americans is sometimes overstated (Mouw and Sobel 2001).

Similarly, partisanship has become increasingly polarized over the last half century. That is, the difference between Republicans and Democrats has been growing ever larger. The majority of voters in the United States identify as either Democrats or Republicans, and they (overwhelmingly) vote for their party's candidate, no matter who that candidate might be or where he or she stands on any particular issue. Partisanship drives electoral outcomes much more than social issues.

If most Americans have become more polarized on the issues of abortion and party identification, their political leaders have become much more polarized on a whole host of issues. One way to see such polarization is by analyzing the way members of Congress have voted. Researchers have developed an index called DW-NOMINATE that statistically measures the ideological positions of political leaders over time, based on the votes they cast in Congress. It uses an algorithm that includes how often conservative legislators vote with other conservatives and not with liberals, as well as how often liberal legislators vote with other liberals and not with conservatives. The larger the DW-NOMINATE score of a particular legislator, the more conservative his or her voting record in Congress. By adding the scores of all Republican legislators together and comparing them with the aggregated scores of all Democratic legislators, we obtain a picture of partisan polarization. Figure 5.2 shows the results, for all sessions of Congress since 1877. The measure of polarization on the horizontal axis simply represents the average difference in DW-NOMINATE scores between Republicans and Democrats. The lower the polarization, the more bi-partisan the voting; the higher the polarization, the more partisan the voting.

As Figure 5.2 shows, party polarization peaked in the early twentieth century, and then steadily declined through the two world wars. Beginning in the 1950s, however, Congress again started to become more partisan. The polarization accelerated rapidly, beginning in the 1980s, and hasn't slowed since (Sinclair 2006). By 2000, Congress was more polarized than at any time in American history since the Civil War.

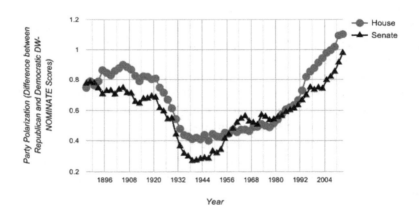

**Figure 5.2** Party Polarization in Congress, 1887–2013.
Source: McCarty and Shor 2015

A complete account of all the causes of this polarization is outside the scope of this book. But the abortion issue has been a critical part of the polarization story, particularly in its rapid acceleration in the 1980s. As Chapter 3 showed, abortion was not considered to be a controversial public issue until at least the 1950s. Legislators, particularly at the state level, had periodically addressed abortion in various discussions, hearings, and statutes before that time, but it was seen as a specialized, technical concern about medical regulation, not a social issue of broad public interest. As abortion became a social issue beginning in the 1960s, and particularly after the 1973 Supreme Court decisions, it was not tied directly to partisan politics. Pro-choice activists were frequently both Democrats and Republicans, and the same was true of pro-life activists.

Nor was it obvious which party would find common cause with which side of the debate. We are accustomed to thinking about abortion rights as almost naturally tied to the Democratic Party while opposition to abortion is connected to the Republican Party. But this has not always been the case. On the eve of the *Roe v. Wade* and *Doe v. Bolton* decisions, the Republican Party had a strong record of support for women's issues. They endorsed the principle of equal pay for equal work before the turn of the century, and endorsed the Equal Rights Amendment four years before the Democrats. Future Republican President George H. W. Bush publicly supported *Roe v. Wade* in the 1970s. By contrast, Democratic leader Jesse Jackson was a fierce opponent, equating abortion with slavery and suggesting legalized abortion would produce a "hell right here on earth" (Jackson 1977). Other Democratic leaders at the time, including Al Gore and Jerry Brown, also held pro-life views (Day 2006). If we shift our focus from political leaders to ordinary Americans, the overall picture is similar. Public opinion polls from the 1970s show consistently more support for abortion rights among Republicans than among Democrats and, conversely, more pro-life sentiment among Democrats than Republicans (Adams 1997).

At the time, it seemed there were solid ideological rationales for this pattern. Modern conservative ideology takes personal freedom as its central organizing principle. Conservative positions on a wide range of issues, from school vouchers and homeschooling, to taxes and Social Security reform, to gun control and healthcare, are formulated in terms of maximizing personal freedom for the individual. Abortion rights fit well within this principle, which perhaps at least partially accounts for why conservatives were initially supportive of the pro-choice position.

Liberalism, by contrast, has long championed the use of state power to protect minority rights, and has sought to give voice to those who are too weak and powerless to speak for themselves. This was the lens through which many liberals initially viewed abortion – the need to protect the vulnerable unborn who cannot speak for themselves. The first presidential campaign ever to center around the abortion issue was that of pro-life activist Ellen McCormack, who ran for the Democratic presidential nomination in 1976 on a pro-life platform. Her effort was popular enough to qualify for public election funding as well as Secret Service protection (Bernstein 1975; Shanahan 1976).

Beyond consistency with these philosophical tenets, the coalitions of voters that made up each political party at the time give reasons to believe the Democrats would come to oppose abortion and Republicans come to support it. As Chapter 3 documented, the pro-life movement, its organization, activists, and arguments, were dominated by Catholics in the 1960s and 1970s. At the same time, Catholics as a whole were one of the Democratic Party's most reliable voting blocs during this period. "To be a Catholic in religion was to be a Democratic in politics," is the way one observer has put it (Prendergast 1999: 23). More than 62 percent of Catholics identified with the Democratic Party in 1973, while only 22 percent identified as Republicans. Even Democratic President Jimmy Carter, an evangelical Protestant, received the majority of Catholic votes (54%) in 1976.

So how did the Republican Party begin to support pro-life and the Democrats pro-choice views? For one thing, conservative Protestants became increasingly important in American politics over this period (Woodberry and Smith 1998). The rise of what came to be called the Christian Right began in the early 1960s and came of age on the national political scene in the 1980s (Oldfield 1996). Demographic changes in the country moved the political center of gravity southward and westward, shifting the balance of power away from the traditional "establishment" elites of the East Coast and incorporating new – more conservative – political ideas into the mainstream (Micklethwait and Wooldridge 2004). Conservative, evangelical Protestants became increasingly important to the electoral fortunes of the Republican Party, and new social issues centering on sexual morality and the family joined the longstanding issue of race in taking front stage in political debates (Layman 1999). American politics were changing during this period, as single-issue advocacy transformed political campaigns and ways of governing (Pierson and Skocpol 2007).

The abortion issue was at the leading edge of this transformation, and its decisive move into partisan politics was made possible by a new cadre of young, conservative leaders that came of age in this period, intent on both shifting the Republican Party to the right, breaking up the near-monopoly Democrats had held on national political power for decades, and transforming a Republican Party long dominated by mainline Protestants who viewed both birth control and abortion as puzzling Catholic obsessions. Four of these young leaders in particular were instrumental in linking the emerging (Protestant) Christian Right with the then (Catholic) pro-life movement: Terry Dolan, Howard Phillips, Richard Viguerie, and Paul Weyrich. All were energetic political entrepreneurs under forty years old. All but Phillips were conservative Catholics who were passionately opposed to abortion. All four also saw the potential for using abortion as a flashpoint to bring more conservative Protestants into the ranks of the Christian Right, and thus into Republican politics. The number of Americans who self-identified as religious evangelicals was similar to today, somewhere between 30 and 40 percent (Smith 1998). They represented a powerful potential political bloc, because of both their numbers and the vast infrastructure of churches, media companies, schools, and other organizations they had built in the preceding decades (Diamond 2000; Jacoby 1998).

Dolan, Phillips, Viguerie and Weyrich met as a group with Jerry Falwell, a key Southern Baptist minister and televangelist, in 1979 and proposed using abortion as the centerpiece of the organizing strategy for a new movement that has come to be called the New Christian Right (McKeegan 1992). Over the course of the 1980s, these leaders used their considerable organizing talents, sizable mailing lists, and the array of organizational infrastructure under their control to begin making opposition to abortion a visible *Republican* issue. Falwell himself first introduced an anti-abortion plan to the Republican national platform at the 1980 convention (Jacoby 1998: 92), less than a decade after the party had publicly supported global population control through family planning and abortion (Critchlow 2007). The Republican Party withdrew its support for an Equal Rights Amendment that same year (Mansbridge 1986). The pro-life movement moved from cutting across party lines to being firmly part of the project to remake and build the Republican Party.

As the pro-life movement was aligning with Republicans, the pro-choice movement, which was tied increasingly tightly to the larger women's movement, was entering the Democratic camp (Carmines, Gerrity, and Wagner 2010; Wolbrecht 2000). Pro-choice forces increasingly insisted that opponents of abortion rights be excluded from the movement and from Democratic organizations. In the 1970s, two feminists – Patricia Goltz and Cathy Callaghan – wanted to continue their feminist activism but were put off by the National Organization of Women's (NOW) endorsement of abortion rights in 1967. Their solution was to found a new organization, Feminists for Life, which would advocate for women's issues such as support for family and medical leave, raising awareness of domestic abuse and opposition to welfare limits, but also oppose legalized abortion. They found it increasingly difficult to maintain their pro-life stance within the larger women's movement. NOW formally revoked Goltz's membership in 1974. As NOW became increasingly tied to the pro-choice movement in the 1980s, their rejection of Feminists for Life hardened further, denying them any formal participation in NOW conferences. Disconnected from the larger women's movement, they drifted into increasingly close connections with the conservative religious pro-life organizations (Kretschmer 2014).

The organizational trajectory of Feminists for Life is a good example of how the issue came to be defined along partisan lines. As the alignment occurred, the pro-life aspect of the group became politically incompatible with the feminist aspect of the group. Something had to give, and eventually Feminists for Life found itself in the orbit of the pro-life movement, giving up its feminist goals in order to preserve its pro-life goals.

Abortion thereby became the fulcrum for a political realignment that has persisted to this day, in much the same way as race transformed American political parties in the 1960s and 1970s (Carmines and Stimson 1989). The abortion issue was a key factor in splitting the traditional Democratic coalition by breaking the bond between the party and Catholic voters (Greenhouse and Siegel 2011; McKenna 2006). Since 1973, Catholic support for Democrats has dropped by 20 percent; today less than half of Catholics identify with the party (see Figure 5.3). Meanwhile, Republican support among Catholics has grown by 72 percent; today almost one third of Catholics identify as Republicans. Abortion was also the banner issue used to mobilize evangelical Protestants to the Republican Party in large numbers throughout the 1980s and 1990s, many of whom had largely stayed away from politics in the past. In 2016, 81 percent of white evangelical Protestants voted for Republican nominee Donald Trump, along with 60 percent of white Catholics (Smith and Martínez 2016). By "flipping" Catholics toward the Republican Party as well as bringing in large numbers of evangelical Protestants, the abortion issue remade American politics.

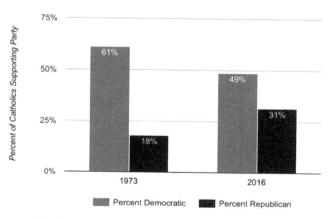

**Figure 5.3** Catholic Partisanship, 1973–2016. Source: created with data from Smith et al. 2017 (General Social Survey variables RELIG and PARTYID)

The capture of the pro-life movement within the orbit of the new Republican coalition, and the move of the pro-choice movement into the Democratic camp, is reflected in changes in public opinion toward abortion. Figure 5.4 shows public support for legal abortion on demand over the last thirty years among those who consider themselves either Republicans or Democrats. The data show little relationship between abortion beliefs and party affiliation in the late 1970s and early 1980s. If anything, Republicans were *more* supportive of abortion rights than were Democrats until at least 1987. In 1977, four years after the Supreme Court legalized abortion, the percentage of Republicans who looked favorably on abortion rights was greater than the percentage of Democrats. Forty years later, Democrats support abortion rights more than Republicans by almost twenty-one percentage points. The picture is roughly similar if we compare the views of self-described liberals with those of conservatives (rather than Democrats and Republicans), as well as if we compare support for abortion under more specific circumstances. In each case, the data show a polarization of public attitudes toward abortion along partisan lines. In an echo of the controversy surrounding the group Feminists for Life decades earlier, a pro-life group called New Wave Feminists was denied a formal partnership in the 2017 Women's March on Washington due to its opposition to abortion (Green 2017).

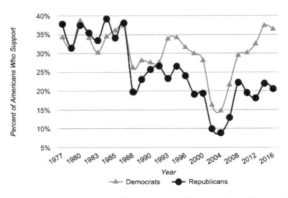

**Figure 5.4** Support for Abortion on Demand, by Party Identification. Source: created with data Smith et al. 2017 (General Social Survey variables ABANY and PARTYID)

The pro-life and pro-choice movements play key roles in the partisan divide. The movements each sought to pursue their agendas through the political process, first through legislation at both state and national levels, and later through the appointment process of judges who are responsible for deciding abortion-related legal cases. Both have long been heavily involved in lobbying efforts at the state and national levels, as well as grooming, choosing, and assisting candidates for public office.

## Abortion and Policy

The pro-life movement enjoyed a string of significant political and legal victories since the 1973 Supreme Court decisions legalizing abortion. It has successfully blocked federal funding for the procedure for poor women since 1976 and helped enact state laws that impose a variety of obstacles to obtaining abortion services, including parental consent statutes, 24-hour waiting periods, and counseling requirements (Donohoe 2005). It has also played a significant role in reducing the availability of both physicians and facilities that provide abortion services. Today, there are less than three hundred abortion clinics nationwide, a number that has declined consistently over the last several decades (Jones and Jerman 2017). Since 2004, state governments have enacted a total of 521 pieces of pro-life legislation that further restricted or regulated access to abortion (NARAL 2017). As has been standard practice for incoming Republican presidents, one of Donald Trump's first executive orders upon assuming the presidency banned US funding of any program or organization that provides or promotes abortion internationally (Hellmann 2017).

The pro-choice movement, for its part, has largely focused on defending the abortion rights established by the *Roe v. Wade* and *Doe v. Bolton* decisions. Pro-choice lobbying and other political efforts, particularly in recent years, have sought to protect the clinical autonomy of physicians and pharmacists to recommend or perform abortion procedures when deemed necessary, as well reduce legal obstacles to women seeking abortions. Since 2004, state governments have enacted a total of 404 pieces of pro-choice legislation that widened access to abortion or other reproductive health services, and increased sex education. Though important, such legislation has had much less impact on abortion access and availability than the new pro-life legislation adopted during the same period. Despite a long string of defeats in the courts over abortion, the movement has continued to battle the pro-life movement in court. In 2016, the Supreme Court decided, in *Whole Woman's Health v. Hellerstadt,* that states could not place significant restrictions on clinics performing abortion in the name of protecting patient health without evidence that such restrictions would actually improve health outcomes (Ford 2016). This decision was the most significant legal victory for the movement in decades.

## Abortion and Identity Politics

Thus far, we have seen how the visibility and sustained mobilization of the pro-choice and pro-life movements have seldom translated directly into determining the outcome of political races. This is in part because abortion was initially not a partisan issue, in part because abortion is not one of the priority issues for most voters, and in part because issues more generally are less important in deciding the outcome of elections than commonly believed. We have also seen that abortion has been a critical driver of the growing faultline between the Republican and Democratic Parties over the last several decades. The pro-life movement and Republican Party have become inextricably intertwined, just as the pro-choice movement has with the Democratic Party. This is due in no small part to the fact that political entrepreneurs brought the movements together with the parties in their pursuit of new coalitions and new advantages in politics. Both movements have also seen political victories, in terms of both legislation supporting their goals, and influence in the legal arena. But the impact of the abortion issue on American politics is greater than any of these individual areas reveals: abortion has become nothing less than a central piece of cultural and political identity in the United States.

Most of the time, we treat the abortion debate as centrally focused on a concrete, specific social issue about which people have different opinions. Politicians generally assume this when they support or oppose legislation that will increase, decrease, or change the availability of abortion services. Reporters generally assume this when they report on controversy surrounding new laws, new court decisions, or new statements by public figures about the issue. Scholarly surveys generally assume this when they seek to estimate the number of people who support or oppose legalized abortion, and under what circumstances. Even the pro-life and pro-choice movements themselves assume this when they try to persuade the public of their goals using different arguments.

There are certainly some cases when this is an accurate way of understanding the abortion debate. But there are far more situations where the debate is less a specific controversy about the various aspects of abortion, and more a general, abstract symbol of an overall worldview. That is, attitudes toward abortion represent differing ways of looking at the world, rather than a well-articulated opinion about medical procedures that terminate pregnancies. The pro-life versus pro-choice debate is not a debate about different points of view; it is a division between different identities and understandings of the world.

The pro-life and pro-choice movements were critical in developing ways of thinking about abortion that led to its central place in larger collective identities. Ginsburg (1998a) identified common activist narratives in her study of both sides of the issue in one midwestern community. Pro-choice activists, she found, use narratives that stress the importance of women working, being involved in other activities outside the home, and playing key roles in the larger culture. Pro-life activists, by contrast, use narratives that stress an acceptance of (and pride in) women's unique role in nurturing families, even as they understand and value a world in which women also work outside the home and are involved in politics. In her study of activists in California, Luker (1984) found that pro-life activists have a worldview in which men and women are intrinsically different, where sexual relationships are sacred and imbued with special meaning, and where moral principles are the same for everyone in a community rather than a matter of personal opinion. Pro-choice activists, by contrast, have a worldview in which men and women are substantially the same, where sexual relationships can have a variety of legitimate meanings, and where a single set of moral principles should not be dictated for everyone in a community. Luker concludes that the beliefs of activists in the pro-life and pro-choice movements "revolve around two very different moral centers" (1984: 186).

These different overarching worldviews (or "moral centers") can be more important than any specific details of the abortion issue itself. And such worldviews have spread from their origins in the two movements to the general population. As Chapter 4 discussed, people describe themselves as "pro-life" or "pro-choice" without having well-formulated, consistent, or even specific opinions about issues that surround the abortion controversy. Abortion is a symbol of the political or cultural "tribe" to which one belongs, and the details of public and medical policy surrounding the procedure are less important.

My own research has shown that identifying with the label "pro-life" ties people to specific beliefs about the abortion issue only if they are activists. Among the general population, being "pro-life" does not necessarily mean one supports banning the procedure, or any of the host of regulations and requirements that might be used to reduce its availability. And being "pro-choice" does not necessarily mean one supports abortion being widely available or supported with government funding (Munson 2009). The important point is not that people vary in their opinions about these details (though they often do), but that many people who consider themselves pro-life or pro-choice have *never thought about these details at all*. A person's side in the abortion controversy signals a commitment to a larger worldview, not a set of concrete opinions about the abortion procedure itself. Claiming an opinion about abortion is to lay claim to a particular identity, not a particular belief about a medical procedure.

Abortion as an identity marker recognizes that the emotions engendered by the abortion debate are key to its impact on politics. On both sides of the issue, abortion is part of the glue Jasper (2011) calls "affective loyalties" that bind people to a group at an emotional level. Passion for or against abortion helps draw boundaries between "us" and "them." It is particularly effective because of the way it ties the passion of the controversy to the moral and emotional differences that people use to define competing worldviews in politics and the larger society (Hunt and Benford 2004; Taylor and Whittier 1992). In social psychological experiments, Mason (2016) has shown how clear divisions (like those present in the abortion debate) help generate both anger and enthusiasm – emotions that help cement loyalty to one worldview while distancing oneself from others. Other research has shown that emotional resonance with political parties – what is called expressive partisanship – is more important than a person's opinions or stance on particular issues in determining their support for a political party (Huddy, Mason, and Aarøe 2015). As the pro-life and pro-choice movements became firmly attached to the Republican and Democratic Parties, the abortion controversy provides the basis for this emotional connection.

As noted earlier, abortion and partisanship stand out as increasingly dividing Americans, even as there has been greater consensus of views on most other issues. As people increasingly agree on the substance of different issues, they have nonetheless separated themselves into different moral worldviews that are symbolically marked by partisanship and the abortion issue. The election of Donald Trump in 2016 was in many ways a stark reminder of the power of partisanship. Trump won the election in large part because millions of Republican voters, who agreed with very few of Trump's policy positions, nonetheless voted for him because he was the Republican nominee. In other words, they saw him as one of "us" and his opponent, Hillary Clinton, as one of "them." And the abortion issue was a central marker of this division, as it has been for decades in political contests at all levels.

Nor did abortion become a central tenet of partisan identity by accident. I outlined earlier in this chapter how specific political actors played a role in moving the pro-life cause to the center of the Republican Party. But larger trends and changes were important, too. The charismatic renewal movement in the Catholic Church, which began in Pittsburgh in 1967 as a reaction to liberalizing trends in the Church (Jacoby 1998), was one important change. It made the melding of more conservative Catholics with evangelical Protestants into a single Republican coalition possible in the face of a long previous history of animosity between Protestants and Catholics. On the Democratic side, the women's movement went from outsiders advocating for change in both parties to a central component of the Democratic Party. This change, in turn, placed the pro-choice position at the center of the party's partisan worldview. The pro-life and pro-choice movements thus came to "anchor" the two parties in the United States (Schlozman 2015).

The connection of abortion to political identity has been made even more important over the last twenty-five years because American courts have backed away from the abortion issue. Court decisions were critical in establishing the terms by which the pro-choice and pro-life movements argued and advocated for their opposing positions. Abortion became an ideological argument about the right to privacy and the rights of women, in no small part because these are the grounds on which the courts had established limits to regulations of the procedure by individual states. Courts were active in defining both the extent of abortion rights demanded by the pro-choice movement and the limitations put on abortion rights demanded by the pro-life movement.

Beginning in the 1980s, however, as abortion was becoming central to partisan political identities, the courts began retreating from the issue by granting greater authority to state legislators to determine the terms of abortion law in each state. This trend culminated in the Supreme Court's 1989 *Webster v. Reproductive Health Services* decision, which did not overturn the 1973 *Roe* decision legalizing abortion, but upheld a series of significant restrictions Missouri placed on abortion procedures in public hospitals and involving government-employed doctors and other medical staff. The *Webster* decision signaled a significant shift in focus from how the courts viewed abortion to how individual voters, through their elected representatives, viewed the issue. This shift "sent shock waves through the political landscape" (Jacoby 1998: 6). The decision "force[d] politicians and voters to confront the issue directly" (Saletan 1998: 115). The battle between the pro-life and pro-choice movements thus shifted from a focus on how the issue was interpreted in elite circles of judges and lawyers to how it fit into the individual and collective identities of ordinary voters.

Soon afterward, the Republican Party began stepping back from the abortion issue too. To be sure, being pro-life continued to root itself at the center of Republican partisanship. But the commitment of the party morphed from active efforts to ban abortion to symbolic support for pro-life identity politics. Individual Republican politicians, and the Republican Party more generally, certainly continued to pursue new regulations and restrictions on abortion that would make it increasingly difficult to seek or perform abortion procedures. But they backed away from calling for banning abortion outright, as they had in the past. "By 1995 every major Republican presidential candidate other than Pat Buchanan had reassured voters that he would not seriously seek a constitutional ban on abortion" (Saletan 1998: 122). The pendulum in Republican politics has more recently swung back again; most of the 2016 contenders for the Republican nomination called explicitly for overturning the 1973 *Roe* decision. The point is that the (vague) principle of being steadfastly pro-life has not changed within the party, even as specific opinions swing back and forth with the political tides. This is because the impact of the abortion debate is most centrally felt as a core part of political identity, not through the specific positions people have about the issue.

## Many Impacts and Meanings

The impact of the ongoing battle between the pro-life and pro-choice movements can be seen in a multitude of ways, on a number of different levels. The controversy is highly visible in many political contests, though its direct impact on the outcome of most elections is limited. Activists in the pro-life and pro-choice movements have been successful in making abortion central to the Democratic and Republican Parties, as well as to many of their political candidates. But voters themselves, for all the passion they show about the issue, seldom use abortion as one of the most important influences in the voting booth. Past voters did not either. In other words, beliefs about abortion are not what matter most in the issue's impact on politics. Instead, it is the way abortion defines the more fundamental notions of "us" versus "them" that is important. Abortion, and which side of the debate one identifies with, helps people define and understand their own political tribe. And in doing so, it has a profound effect on the partisanship and divisions that dominate not just election contests, but also larger social and cultural dynamics.

This impact relates back to the central concern of the book. Abortion is not simply a social issue, with various complexities and connections to other issues and concerns. Instead, the meaning of abortion has changed over time. As Chapter 2 revealed, abortion was once used in the nineteenth century by physicians to professionalize and convince political elites and the public that they had specialized medical knowledge not available to others. This chapter revealed how abortion was once again used in the twentieth century by political entrepreneurs seeking to change the coalitions that defined the two major parties. Its meaning changed, as it came to represent a particular political worldview rather than a specific set of attitudes toward a medical procedure. In this way, the abortion issue is not simply part of the political debate; it is part of defining American politics itself.

# 6

## *American Exceptionalism*

The debate over abortion is of course not just limited to the United States. Public opinion is divided on the issue throughout the world. There exists a great deal of variation in the legal status of the procedure; it is outlawed in some countries no matter what the circumstances, but in others it is legal in all circumstances and sometimes subsidized by the government. The United States falls somewhere in the middle in terms of both the level of public support for abortion and the laws governing it. But what makes the United States unique in the world is the sustained level of public controversy surrounding the abortion issue. Although people continue to disagree about abortion around the world, only in the United States is it a central, recurring issue in politics at all levels of government. And only in the United States does it remain a cultural touchstone around which moral understandings more generally revolve.

This chapter explores the reasons for this American exceptionalism. It first outlines how the US stands out from the rest of the world. Then, it reviews the three main dynamics that have led to this difference. First, there is an *institutional* dynamic in which different kinds of political structures have allowed the controversy to persist while it was largely settled elsewhere. Second, there is an *ideological* dynamic in which the abortion controversy has been fed by the long tradition of distinctive moral politics in the United States. Finally, there is an *historical* dynamic in which abortion has remained politically and culturally salient in the

US by changes in what the issue symbolized and meant in public discussion. Together, these three dynamics have sustained the close attention paid to the abortion issue in the United States even as it has faded in importance elsewhere in the world.

## *Setting the United States Apart*

Chapter 4 explored the overall attitudes toward abortion of Americans as well as some of the complexities in their beliefs about the issue. The overall levels of support and opposition to abortion among Americans are not particularly distinctive. The liberalization of abortion law happened in many countries beginning in the 1960s (Glendon 1987), often tied to a growing acceptance of women's rights (Boyle, Kim, and Longhofer 2015). US public opinion about the issue is about as divided as public opinion in many countries. Across the fifty-nine countries that participated in the latest World Values Survey (2016), fifty have a greater proportion of the population who say that abortion is never justifiable; fifty-three have a greater proportion of the population who say that abortion is always justifiable. Roughly speaking, the split between pro-choice and pro-life views in the United States is approximately the same as the split in views in countries like Spain, Germany, New Zealand, and Australia. A more recent poll (Ipsos 2016) showed the United States right in the middle of the twenty-three countries studied in terms of public support for abortion, with countries like Italy, China, Japan, Russia, Mexico and Brazil showing less public support for allowing abortion whenever a woman decides she wants one, and countries like Canada, South Korea, Germany, Spain, Great Britain, and France showing more support.

The legal status of abortion varies widely within the United States, as each of the fifty states has a different set of laws. Nonetheless, the series of US Supreme Court rulings relating to abortion since 1973 has set the broad parameters within which all these laws operate. States may not prohibit abortion outright, but they are permitted to add a wide variety of restrictions and regulations on abortion that can make it difficult for most women to obtain them. Some states, such as Vermont, place few such restrictions. Other states, such as Oklahoma, place many. This is similar to the status of abortion law elsewhere in the world. Like the United States, the rules governing abortion vary in Mexico on a state by state basis. Abortion is illegal in all or almost all circumstances in countries such as El Salvador, Senegal, Ireland, and the Philippines. By contrast, there are few legal limits to the procedure in countries such as Great Britain, Sweden, and China. Other countries, like Germany, are similar to the United States in allowing for a significant number of abortions, but also putting in place significant legal restrictions (Ferree 2003).

In terms of both attitudes and laws, the United States is not on either extreme compared with many other places around the world. What does differ, however, is the visibility and importance of the issue in the United States over a long period of time, as well as the level of contentiousness between pro-life and pro-choice supporters. The abortion debate flares up around the world, often raised by a particular incident or event. In Brazil, for example, the mosquito-born Zika virus led to a flurry of interest and debate over abortion in 2015 and 2016 after it was discovered that the virus causes birth defects when pregnant women become infected. Brazil prohibits abortions except in cases of rape or when a pregnancy threatens a woman's life, a legal status that is seldom subject to public discussion. But the Zika epidemic led to a period of social concern and debate over the issue. Some Brazilians called for greater legal access to abortion to deal with the effects of the virus, and others called for even stricter enforcement of the law to better uphold the existing prohibition against abortion in cases of birth defects (Carless 2016). Whatever side Brazilians took on this issue, the debate itself was short-lived, tied specifically to the epidemic.

In the United States, by contrast, abortion is continuously at the forefront of public debate and discussion, with or without a triggering incident. The amount of press coverage is a good indication of the visibility of the abortion issue. In 2016, the *New York Times* published 975 articles that mentioned abortion.

By contrast, the *Times of India* published only 409; *The Daily Telegraph* in London, only 138. Both the pro-life and pro-choice movements remain at high levels of mobilization at all times in the United States, ensuring that the issue stays in front of the public in ways that it does not in other countries. Moreover, the abortion debate is now embedded in political and cultural institutions in ways that guarantee ongoing attention. But this begs the question of why movement mobilization and the issue's connection to political and cultural institutions differ so much in the United States than in other countries. The remainder of this chapter provides an explanation.

# The Institutional Causes

## Access Points

As all US students learn from elementary school onward, the United States government is structured by the US Constitution into three separate branches: legislative, executive, and judicial. Moreover, governance is federated, meaning that these different branches are also divided into national, state, and local levels. All of this adds up to governance in which political power and decision-making are fragmented. No one arm of government, and no one level, is able to completely control political outcomes on its own.

The fragmentation of power translates into many different points of opportunity for those interested in influencing government policy. These are called "access points" by political scientists, a term which refers to the multiple forums through which people might try to change public policy (Ehrlich 2011; Steinmo 1989). In the legislative branch, there are periodic elections of officials, from school board members and code enforcement officers at the local level, through county commissioners, state legislators, up to senators and representatives in Congress. Interested parties can try to influence the outcome of elections at each of these levels. But they can also access each of these levels after elections, through lobbying, petitioning, and other forms of influence. If they are unsuccessful in accomplishing their goals through the access points in the legislative branch, they can also influence policy through the judicial branch through lawsuits and other forms of judicial pressure (including, in many states, the ability to elect judges). The executive branch also provides many access points, as interested parties can approach civil servants and others that work in government agencies at all levels by providing reports, attending public hearings, and so forth.

As a result of these many access points, the fragmented US political system makes it difficult for any given issue to be settled once and for all. No matter what choices the decision-makers at one level or one arm of the government make, those who are unhappy with the decision can always use other access points to try and counter those decisions. Chapter 4 highlighted how this has played out in the case of the pro-life and pro-choice movements in the United States. The history of the abortion debate has really been one in which the two movements battled each other at many different points of access to government policy. The pro-choice movement won a major victory in the judicial branch, most notably the 1973 *Roe v. Wade* and *Doe v. Bolton* Supreme Court decisions, after which the pro-life movement won a series of victories in the legislative branch, by passing a long series of increasingly restrictive laws that limit the scope and availability of the abortion services legalized by the courts. The mass media, controlled by a variety of private, competitive interests rather than the state, offer still further opportunities for political influence that have been embraced by both movements. The battle between the two movements has been extended indefinitely by the wide availability of access points that each movement uses to push its agenda.

This back-and-forth also implies an important quality of access points; they constitute veto points by which one side in the debate can limit or reverse the gains made by the other. The 1973 Supreme Court decisions represented a significant victory for the pro-choice movement, legalizing abortion at the national level and invalidating all the state-level restrictions on the procedure that existed at the time. As the highest judicial body, there was no direct way for the pro-life movement to respond or appeal within the judicial branch. But they could use other access points to limit the effect of the Supreme Court decision. They were successful at the national legislative level in getting the Hyde Amendment passed in 1977, eliminating federal funding for abortion services. At the state legislative level, the pro-life movement supported passage of a variety of new laws restricting access to abortion beginning immediately after the 1973 Supreme Court decisions. The pro-life movement was thus able to limit the scope of the pro-choice victory following the legalization of abortion (Soper 1994).

A more recent example comes from the increasing number of restrictions that states have placed on health clinics that provide abortions, many of which are different from requirements for any other type of healthcare. In 2013, the pro-life movement was successful in having two new such restrictions placed on clinics in Texas, one requiring physicians performing abortions to have admitting privileges at a local hospital and the other requiring that clinics meet the same safety standards as hospital operating rooms. Supporters and opponents of these new restrictions alike predicted that they would be impossible to meet for a substantial number of abortion providers in the state. This meant the closure of those clinics and a substantial victory for the pro-life movement at the state legislative level. The pro-choice movement responded by challenging these restrictions in court, ultimately leading to a 2016 Supreme Court decision overturning the new Texas law as unconstitutional (Ford 2016). In this case, pro-life victories were undone by the pro-choice movement by using access points to the judicial branch to reverse decisions made in the legislative branch. Access points thus become veto points by which one side can deny the other victory.

Many political systems are organized in such a way that public policy decisions, once made, reduce or eliminate the public controversy surrounding them. They become settled. This does not mean that everyone agrees with the policy or that opponents do not continue to look for opportunities to change it, but such opportunities are limited and the focus of policymakers and the public alike turns to other issues. In Britain, for example, abortion policy is not set by local jurisdictions in the same way it is in the United States; they have a single national policy. By contrast, the many access points – and thus veto points – in the American system make it difficult for a public policy decision to become the stable status quo because they allow partisans on both sides many more opportunities to push alternatives and keep the issue in the public eye.

# The American Medical Association

The formal (and fragmented) structure of the US political system is an important part of the institutional explanation, but there are other key institutions as well. Chief among them is the American Medical Association (AMA). Chapter 2 outlined the importance of the AMA as a critical supporter of criminalizing abortion for the first time in the nineteenth century. At that time, the AMA was a fledgling organization that saw abortion as a way to differentiate the specialized medical knowledge of university-trained physicians from others offering healthcare. By the time abortion became a public, and politicized, issue in the 1960s and early 1970s, the AMA had become the largest, most important, and most powerful trade group and lobbying organization for physicians in the United States.

The AMA is important to the continued debate over abortion because of its unwillingness to take a firm stand on the issue in this later period. As the primary collective voice of America's doctors, the AMA maintained two critical and longstanding organizational objectives during the period of the 1973 Supreme Court decisions: (1) maintain or increase the high salaries of its members, and (2) maintain or increase the freedom of its members to make medical decisions without outside interference (in other words, maintain the clinical autonomy of doctors). They faced a coalescence of different threats to this first goal in the 1970s. Government officials, business leaders, insurance companies, and public reformers had come together during this time to push for national health insurance, which would greatly expand the government regulations shaping the prices paid to doctors for medical care. With conservative Republican President Richard Nixon as well as the National Governor's Association also in support of such a program, national health insurance looked like a real possibility (Halfmann 2011: 83). The concern of the AMA was particularly acute because they had fought against, and lost, the creation of the Medicare program in 1965, which had put the state in charge of determining some of the costs of medical procedures for the first time.

As the abortion issue took on increasing public prominence, the AMA's second major objective also came into focus: clinical autonomy. An important part of the professionalization of medical care that occurred in the nineteenth century was the establishment of trained physicians as the primary gatekeepers of medical knowledge and expertise. Physicians were largely in control of their own workplaces, free from direct supervision, and empowered to make whatever decisions they deemed appropriate when it came to both patients and other healthcare workers such as nurses and hospital staff (Freidson 1970; Hafferty and Light 1995). Doctors value clinical autonomy to practice medicine without outside judgment of their decisions by government officials, politicians, hospital administrators, and insurance companies. The abortion issue threatened the clinical autonomy of doctors by taking abortion decisions out of their hands and putting them in the hands of non-medical decision-makers such as politicians, judges, and voters. For the AMA, increasing legislative restrictions on abortion were an unwelcome intrusion on the clinical autonomy of doctors. At the same time, the AMA's membership, like the general public, was divided on the abortion issue, and eliminating all laws governing abortion shifted some of the medical judgment historically left to doctors to their (pregnant, female) patients.

The AMA's interest in preserving high salaries and clinical autonomy were both under pressure at the time when the abortion issue was gaining steam in the 1960s and early 1970s. Faced with prioritizing the core interests of physicians, the AMA chose to focus its attention and political power on preserving the economic prerogatives of doctors (Reinhardt 1988). Clinical autonomy remained an interest of the group, but it was not prioritized as highly as financial advantage. And ultimately the AMA was willing to give up some clinical autonomy if it meant preserving or expanding the economic position of its member physicians. In the case of the abortion issue, the AMA was not centrally involved in the debate over abortion as it came increasingly into the public spotlight in the 1960s and 1970s. The AMA first avoided the issue, then took a tepid stand in favor of limited reform in 1967, after several states had already liberalized their abortion laws. They passed another vague and ambiguous resolution concerning abortion in 1970 (Halfmann 2011). At this time, the AMA was focused on defeating national healthcare proposals and keeping its members unified, rather than taking a strong stand on abortion. Its attention was simply elsewhere.

This decision had important effects on how the issue developed in the United States. Sociologist Drew Halfmann (2011) has studied the way abortion law in the United States was shaped differently than in Canada and Great Britain, two other English-speaking democracies with a common legal ancestry. Halfmann focused on the different ways in which the central medical associations in each country reacted to the issue. The group representing doctors in all three (the AMA in the United States, the CMA in Canada, and the BMA in Great Britain) opposed both extremes of banning all abortions and allowing abortion on demand. But from these common positions, they followed very different strategies based on their position within each country's political and economic institutions. In both Canada and Great Britain, the economic privileges of doctors had already been largely curtailed by national health insurance programs. As a result, the CMA and the BMA focused a great deal of energy on a core issue that they could still control: clinical autonomy. They engaged directly with the abortion issue and put their full weight behind compromise abortion laws that preserved the prerogatives of doctors as abortion-procedure gatekeepers.

In the United States, by contrast, the AMA prioritized continued defense of economic privileges and made clinical autonomy less of a priority (Halfmann 2003). As a result, American doctors continue to earn substantially more money than their Canadian and British counterparts. Average remuneration for medical specialists in the United States in 2004 was $230,000 annually, but only $161,000 in Canada and $150,000 in Great Britain. The difference for general practitioners is similar (Peterson and Burton 2007). But the AMA also played an inconsistent and ambivalent role in the debate over abortion, never putting its full weight behind a particular position. This ambivalence initially contributed to a more liberal abortion law in the United States than in the other two countries (though this is no longer the case). But more importantly, it allowed the abortion issue to drift further outside the medical domain, where it could become more politicized and publicly contentious. By comparison, the abortion issue has a more settled status in Canada and Great Britain despite continued divisions of public opinion, because doctors in these countries took a greater interest in keeping the abortion issue as a medical issue.

The AMA continues this focus on economic concerns over issues of clinical autonomy to this day. For example, seven out of the nine of its "Legislative Priorities" in 2017 focus on financial issues in medical care (the remaining two focus on cybersecurity and the opioid epidemic). Clinical autonomy is not even mentioned (American Medical Association 2017). This focus has allowed the pro-life movement to push for increasing legislation that directly impacts the way physicians practice medicine. Ten states, for example, require abortion providers to conduct an ultrasound on every patient and offer her the opportunity to view the images. Four states require that the provider both show and describe ultrasound images to every patient (Guttmacher Center). Five other states mandate providers to read statements about fetal pain to all patients (Tobin 2008). Such legislation is opposed by the AMA as well as other American physician groups, such as the American College of Obstetricians and Gynecologists. In 2012, leaders of five major medical groups (though not the AMA) published an editorial in the influential *New England Journal of Medicine* decrying the encroachment of politics on clinical autonomy, including physician autonomy around abortion procedures (Weinberger et al. 2012). But such opposition continues to be at the periphery of the work done by the AMA and other medical associations. The absence of their medical leadership on the issue provides space for both sides to continue to mobilize around abortion as a political concern rather than a medical one. At the same time, it has allowed abortion services to become marginalized within the medical community itself (Joffe 1996).

## Political Parties

If the American Medical Association is one important part of the institutional explanation for American exceptionalism on the abortion issue, the structure and role of political parties in the United States is another. Just as there are many access points in the formal American political process, there are also more points of access to the two major parties. And the openness of the parties to outside influence has changed the nature of the debate over abortion. To see this, we can continue to take advantage of Halfmann's (2011) comparison of the issue in the United States, Canada, and Great Britain. In addition to the many other similarities between the three countries, they also share a political arena in which a small number of major parties dominate (two in both the United States and Great Britain, three in Canada).

Chapter 5 addressed the way abortion has become more than just an issue addressed by the Democratic and Republican Parties; it has become a central organizing principle around which the parties are organized and an increasingly important litmus test of party orthodoxy and commitment. The central role of abortion in the political parties corresponds to a central role of abortion in political debate and elections at all levels of government. This pattern has not happened in the major British and Canadian parties. Why not?

One important factor is the ease with which interest groups can become involved in party politics in the United States (Thomas

2001). Party nominees for elections are decided by primaries and caucuses that allow wide public participation, including in some cases voters who are not even part of the party. The policy positions (that is, the party platforms) are similarly established at conventions where a broad range of people within the party are given a voice. At the same time, however, relatively few citizens actually make use of this openness and actively participate in party politics. Together, these two factors mean that small groups of particularly committed activists can have a strong impact on which candidates are nominated for office, as well as the formal ideological position of the party on a particular issue. The short history of the Tea Party movement shows how quickly such influence can be established. From its origins in 2008, the Tea Party quickly became a major voice in Republican party politics, replacing more traditional Republican candidates in elections at all levels of government, shaping the issues championed by the party, and establishing a Tea Party caucus in Congress all within just a few years.

The Tea Party itself was an important source of leverage for the pro-life movement too. Early Tea Party spokespeople frequently downplayed social issues such as gay marriage and abortion in describing the goals of the movement. But activists themselves were drawn principally (though not exclusively) from the now-longstanding conservative base of the Republican Party, including many who had long been involved in partisan politics (Abramowitz 2011; Arceneaux and Nicholson 2012). The Tea Party's growing dominance in the Republican Party provided a window of opportunity to elect particularly conservative candidates, who then worked to implement many of the pro-life movement's goals. Tea Party activists who were pro-choice largely held their tongues (Skocpol and Williamson 2012: 168). New legislative efforts to restrict abortion, as well as the mobilization by the pro-choice movement to resist such efforts, was thus intensified by the growth of the Tea Party.

In Great Britain, by contrast, parties are largely insulated from outside social movements. Party nominees for elections are decided by a small group of dues-paying party insiders, making it difficult for outside groups to break in with their own candidates. Party platforms are similarly determined by party insiders, not by party conventions involving thousands of delegates. Canadian parties are somewhat more open than those in Great Britain, allowing outsiders to sometimes have a voice (Halfmann 2011: 135), but they are still far more restricted than their American counterparts. The greater barriers to outside participation make it more difficult and less likely for single-issue advocates from outside the party to impact its choice of politicians and positions.

Despite the extraordinary levels of partisanship in American politics today, the party loyalty of individual politicians is still far less than in many other countries. In the US, elections tend to be candidate-focused, and both fundraising and staffing of campaigns is managed by candidates themselves. As a result, American political candidates often rely on social movements that support them for assistance with these critical tasks. By contrast, in Great Britain and Canada, elections are much more party-focused. Voters choose parties more than they do individual politicians, and election campaigns are financed and staffed by the parties themselves rather than individual candidates. Once elected, American politicians make individual choices about how to vote on any particular bill or piece of legislation, and can even introduce their own policy proposals. Very often they vote for the position of their party, but they are not required to do so. In Canada and Great Britain, the party itself initiates most policy proposals, and legislators are required, with few special exceptions known as "free votes," to vote in the way their party directs.

These differences have allowed the pro-life and pro-choice movements to make abortion a central issue for American political parties. Using the many access points available to both parties, as well as the ability to directly support and influence individual Democratic and Republican candidates, the movements have come to "anchor" (Schlozman 2015) the party system in the United States. This has contributed to keeping the abortion issue part of the public debate for decades. By contrast, the major political parties in both Canada and Great Britain have been able to limit the politicization of abortion. Since 1967, for example, no ruling party in Great Britain has proposed a bill or taken an official position on abortion (Halfmann 2011: 138), and it has only rarely been raised by parties in Canada. The party system in the United States thus contributes to the larger set of institutional causes for the exceptional position abortion holds in American public life.

## *The Ideological Causes*

American political institutions help to explain American exceptionalism, but ideological dynamics contribute as well. The levels of mobilization around abortion are high because people's passions surrounding the issue are high; and these have their antecedents in the moralistic approach to politics that has characterized much of American history and today's contemporary political culture. A culture of moralism has helped to draw the battle lines over abortion especially brightly, and made crossing them, or even letting them rest, more difficult.

As Chapter 2 described, abortion was not always a moral issue in itself. It became so only in the nineteenth century, and only in response to a variety of social changes. Without this change, abortion might continue to be debated as just another medical procedure; that is, it would not sustain the same level or depth of passion as it does today. After all, we do not have large social movements mobilizing around other medical procedures, such as heart-bypass surgery or vasectomies. Even those aspects of medical care that touch on some of the same issues as abortion, including sexuality and human birth and death, do not engender the same level of passion. There are certainly differences of opinion, for example over sterilization, fertility treatments, Caesarean sections, and end-of-life care, but none generates even a small fraction of the debate (or vitriol) of the pro-life and pro-choice movements surrounding abortion.

Many observers have pointed out that abortion has remained more fully grounded in medical discussions outside of the United States. "In Europe the debate about abortion is conducted in medical rather than moral terms," say Micklethwait and Wooldridge (2004: 311), continuing, "For Americans, abortion can seemingly never be just about health. It has to be a clash of absolutes." Though they may exaggerate the contrast between Europe and the US (abortion is strongly tinged by moral concern in Europe too), the basic point they make is correct: Americans tie abortion more tightly to moral beliefs than do citizens in many other places.

On his way to the New World from England in 1630, John Winthrop shared with his fellow Puritan settlers aboard the ship *Arbella* his ideas for a new colony that would be a model of Christian charity. "We shall be as a city on a hill," he declared, "the eyes of all people are upon us" (Bremer 2003). Winthrop would go on to be governor of the Massachusetts Bay Colony and his words have been frequently cited for three and a half centuries to invoke the idea that the United States possesses a moral character that is unique in the world. Many subsequent observers would go on to make the same observation, emphasizing in particular the special focus Americans give to issues of morality. Alexis de Tocqueville, perhaps the most well-known observer of the character of America, said in his nineteenth-century explanation for the strength of American democracy that "Christianity … reigns without any obstacle, by universal consent; the consequence is … that every principle of the moral world is fixed and determinate" (De Tocqueville 2009 [1835]: 562). Almost a century later, English writer G. K. Chesterton described the United States as possessing "the soul of a church" (1922: 12).

The United States has had a long history of morality politics. Abortion is not the first policy issue to have become a moral issue. There have been previous battles over witchcraft, slavery, alcohol, immigrants, communists, civil rights and, most recently, terrorism that have all taken on the character of moral crusades. American politics "constantly gets entangled in two vital urges – redeeming "us" and reforming "them"," concludes political scientist James Morone (2004: 3). The political culture of the country adds a moral dimension to many controversies that is greater and more central than the political controversies elsewhere. In doing so, issues become more divisive, more difficult to resolve, and thus more longstanding. The pro-life and pro-choice movements have both drawn on the same moralistic political culture as their predecessors in earlier political fights to make abortion a defining issue of the contemporary American political and social landscape. And the result is a bigger, more long-standing, and more divisive battle over the issue.

The historical tradition of morality politics may be caused in part by the lack of clear social class distinctions in the United States. Many societies offer clear markers of social position, and divisions between "worthy" and "unworthy," or "privileged" and "unprivileged," or "us" and "them" are predetermined and easily identified. Social class plays no less an important role in the United States, but the markers of class are more ambiguous and less agreed upon. As a result, Americans look to the alternative of *moral* worth as a basis for classifying people into "us" and "them." America's status as a nation of immigrants contributes to this tendency. Ethnic background is an important marker in only some cases and not others, and how ethnic differences map onto status divisions in American culture is frequently changing. Because American society is so open and fluid in comparison to many others, moral politics takes on an increased importance.

But we do not have to limit the ideological explanation for American exceptionalism simply to past history. The moral landscape of the contemporary United States reflects and reinforces this culture. This is most apparent in the high levels of religious faith and practice. The United States is a very religious place, and Americans express levels of religious faith, attendance at religious services, and participation in prayer and other religious devotions at much higher rates than in other places around the world. Almost two-thirds of Americans say that they are "absolutely sure" of the existence of God and even more (72%) have the same certainty about the existence of heaven. More than three out of four Americans say they pray at least every week; over half say they pray every day or more. And over a third say they attend religious services once a week or more. Overall, more than three quarters say that religion is important to them (Pew Research Center 2015). The numbers reported in surveys of religious belief and behavior vary somewhat from year to year and survey to survey, but overall the picture is clear: religion, and the Christian tradition in particular (only about 5% of Americans identify with a non-Christian religion), remains an extraordinarily important aspect of American life.

The high levels of religiosity are a surprise to many people, who have long held on to the conventional wisdom that the US is a largely secular country. This confusion comes in part because religious beliefs and behavior *have* declined in recent years. But this is a relatively recent trend (Putnam and Campbell 2010), and religious belief and practice were at such high levels previously that even fairly substantial rates of decline still leave the country an extremely religious place. The confusion also stems from the lack of an outside reference point. Many Americans might look around and see the role of religion shrinking from the lives of their communities. But compared to many other countries, and particularly other industrialized democracies, religion in the United States remains extremely important. The countries where people attend religious services less frequently than Americans include Italy, Canada, Great Britain, Germany, France, Japan, and Sweden. Even citizens of Iran report less religious service attendance (Putnam and Campbell 2010: 9). In the United States, only three percent of Americans say they do not believe in God, compared to six percent in Israel, 15 percent in Australia, 18 percent in Great Britain, and 23 percent in France (Smith 2012).

This relatively high level of religiosity translates into regular reminders for many Americans of the importance of moral concerns and distinctions in their daily lives. In comparison with citizens in other countries, there are more opportunities for Americans to connect political (or medical or social) debates to moral divisions. There is also a greater availability of moral language, metaphors, and lessons that make it easier for, and increase the likelihood of, a controversy to develop into a moral crusade. Micklethwait and Wooldridge note that the United States is "marinated in religion," which encourages Americans to see social issues in terms of individual virtues and vices (2004: 382). And once a particular "type" of person or behavior becomes a moral virtue or vice, the controversy increases and the possibilities for a final settlement of an issue go down.

For many observers of the abortion debate, religion is assumed to explain one side of the controversy more than the other. The pro-life movement is indeed connected to high levels of religious faith among politically conservative groups. But the role of religion in explaining the exceptional nature of the abortion debate is not limited to just the pro-life side. As Chapter 5 described, abortion has become a central litmus test around which the coalitions of the Republican and Democratic Parties are organized. A full 85 percent of Republicans identify as religious, which is consistent with the idea that religion is particularly important to the pro-life side of the debate. But 71 percent of Democrats also identify as religious, which is still a large majority within the pro-choice party (Pew Research Center 2015). Churches and other religious institutions are more central to today's pro-life movement than they are to the pro-choice movement too, but this hasn't always been the case. As Chapter 2 described, religious leaders and clergy were central players in building the pro-choice movement in the mid-twentieth century. Pro-choice presidential candidate Barack Obama said in 2008 that "those who diminish the moral elements of the [abortion] decision aren't expressing the full reality of it" (Pulliam and Olsen 2008). Religious viewpoints, institutions, and individuals are thus tied to the controversy on both sides.

The ideological basis of the abortion debate in the United States has been part of the foundation for some of the most extreme elements of the pro-life movement in particular. Those who have engaged in anti-abortion violence have done so from a commitment to moral certainty of their cause and in the name of their religious beliefs. The prophetic tradition of the Old Testament has been an important part of social movements advocating reform throughout American history (Darsey 1999). And this pattern has continued through to the abortion debate. Following the 9/11 terrorist attacks, Jerry Falwell, the well-known televangelist and key architect of making abortion a partisan issue, tied the tragedy directly to the abortion debate, saying "the abortionists have got to bear some burden for this because God will not be mocked. And when we destroy 40 million little innocent babies, we make God mad" (Morone 2004: 488). Pat Robertson, standing next to him, agreed. Though both men later apologized for the remarks, the episode nonetheless demonstrates the exceptional ideological fervor with which the battle over abortion continues to be waged across the United States.

## The Historical Causes

A third source of American exceptionalism is the historical flexibility of the abortion issue and what it has represented in public debate in the United States. This goes to the central argument of the book: that abortion has been a remarkably flexible symbol of a wide variety of social and political anxieties. The terms over which the abortion debate has been engaged, as well as the constituencies for each side, have varied as the social and political landscape has changed.

This historical flexibility is an important part of the reason why the abortion issue has not been put to rest in the United States over the last half century. Even as some of the social and cultural divides in the country have shifted, they have brought abortion along, reinterpreting and reimagining the meaning of the abortion debate in order to use it as both an explanation and symbol for a particular point of view. The very elasticity of the abortion debate, its ability to take on different meanings at different points in time, is a key part of its staying power in the American public consciousness.

These changing meanings have been raised throughout the previous chapters. They begin with the first efforts to criminalize abortion, spearheaded by physicians seeking to professionalize. These early calls to identify abortion in criminal statutes and forbid abortion procedures outside a physician's care were made salient to other elites in part by growing nativism in the country. There was concern that white, native-born women were most likely to seek out abortions. Although the pro-life and pro-choice movements as we understand them today did not exist at the time, the discussion over abortion was in part a discussion about immigration and race. Several decades later, abortion was criminalized but still widely practiced, including openly run clinics and mass media advertising, at a time of high levels of immigration and accelerating urbanization. The meaning of abortion shifted in these discussions, focusing on the connection that some saw to public disorder and the "unwashed masses" of immigrants.

In the mid-twentieth century, the increased status of physicians, along with scientific advancements and greatly improved medical care, led to a push to liberalize the strict abortion statutes enacted in the previous century. Physicians wanted greater discretion in making abortion decisions, while medical advances made abortion a safer option than childbirth for the first time in history. On the other side, the Catholic Church, now a fully established part of the American social and religious landscape, strongly opposed liberalizing abortion laws and in doing so sowed the seeds of today's pro-life movement. And the issue of race was raised repeatedly, with the specter of abortion being the newest weapon against African-Americans and other minority groups. The meaning of abortion thus shifted during this period to questions of medical autonomy, religion, and race.

As the issue became increasingly politicized in the 1960s and early 1970s, the terrain of the abortion debate changed again, this time to issues of sexuality and the increased mobilization of the women's movement. Those in favor of abortion rights emphasized their centrality to equality for women and increasingly celebrated a growing openness to sexual activity not bounded by lifelong marriage and desire for children. Those opposed to abortion rights expressed concern about changes to the family brought about by the greater equality of women, including their participation in the labor force, as well as the socially (and morally) destructive effects of sexual activity unfettered by the potential consequences of pregnancy (Back 1987). These were by no means the only issues on which the pro-choice and pro-life movements mobilized. But they were the dominant sides of an increasingly politicized debate over abortion during this period.

Beginning in the 1980s, abortion became increasingly associated with partisan politics. Pro-choice views became a central organizing tenet of the Democratic coalition, while pro-life views became core to the Republican one. Abortion became part of a larger debate between parties that were increasingly divided by ideological conflict. Abortion rights came to represent a commitment to liberalism, while abortion restrictions represented a commitment to conservatism. Abortion rights represented an openness to different lifestyles and an appreciation of diversity, while abortion restrictions represented defense of the traditional family and a desire for smaller government. In the political context of polarizing parties, the *Roe v. Wade* decision legalizing abortion came to symbolize a larger conservative concern with (undemocratic) judicial interference and overreach. The previous meanings of abortion did not go away, but they faded in importance relative to these new concerns. The American experience with the abortion debate is exceptional in part because other countries have not experienced the same history of shifting meanings and symbols surrounding the procedure.

None of the arguments raised by the pro-life or pro-choice movements in the United States are unique; the same arguments are made throughout the world. Nor are elements of American institutional arrangements, party politics, political culture, and religiosity entirely absent elsewhere. But the abortion debate has been politically and socially important in the United States longer, involved far greater mobilizations by social movements on both sides, shaped the passions of more people on a more sustained basis, and had a greater impact on American political development than elsewhere around the world. There are institutional, ideological, and historical factors that account for this exceptional American experience. They ensure that the battle over abortion in the United States will continue to look different there from anywhere else.

# 7

## *Stability and Change in Abortion Politics*

"Well I think it's terrible ... [I]n the ninth month, you can take the baby and rip the baby out of the womb of the mother just prior to the birth of the baby," declared Donald Trump, in the final debate before being elected President (Woolley and Peters 2016). His graphic depiction of abortion echoed that of Carly Fiorina, who in a debate a month earlier dared abortion rights supporters to "watch a fully formed fetus on the table, its heart beating, its legs kicking while someone says we have to keep it alive to harvest its brain. This is about the character of our nation" (Beckwith 2015). Both are false descriptions of legal abortion, but nonetheless reflect the particular way Republicans have taken up the pro-life banner.

On the other side of the abortion debate, pro-choice politicians identify any attempt to restrict or limit funding for abortion services as part of a "war on women." Cecile Richards, the executive director of Planned Parenthood, expressed concern over "hateful rhetoric and harassment and intimidation of both doctors and women ... It's really un-American" (Inskeep 2015). During the 2016 presidential election, Hillary Clinton argued that the "extreme views about women" held by pro-life politicians were the same as those held by some terrorist groups (Merica 2015).

These characterizations illustrate a number of important features of the debate over abortion in America today. The debate has spread far beyond activists in the pro-life and pro-choice movements. The abortion issue is one about which the majority of Americans have an opinion, many of which are very *strong* opinions. Perhaps more importantly, people are *expected* to have an opinion, even if they know very little personally about the procedure or the issue. The comments illustrate how the abortion debate – whatever other meanings it might have – has become a defining aspect of American politics. Political candidates, from the President all the way down to local officials, are *expected* to speak about the issue, even if it is not a central part of their campaign or one of the central issues of interest to the public in an election. A candidate's view of abortion is a critical component of his or her identification with either the Republican or Democratic Party. The comments also show how little complexity or nuance is permitted in discussions of the abortion issue. The many shades of gray that might be involved in formulating informed attitudes about the abortion procedure itself in medicine, the women who seek abortion, or the appropriate public policies that might regulate it, are all buried in stark, black-and-white visions of what abortion *means* or *represents*. Finally, this abortion rhetoric shows how far apart people are on this issue. They suggest that there is no middle ground.

But it has not always been this way. This book has traced the evolution of the abortion debate through the course of American history, and particularly through American politics and both the pro-life and pro-choice movements. The central theme of this evolution is that the cultural and political meaning of abortion has never been fixed, but has changed based on the changing divides in the American social fabric. This capacity for layered and shifting meanings is the key to the level of controversy and its staying power as a public issue.

## *Where We Have Been*

As Chapter 2 showed, abortion was neither illegal, rare, nor controversial in the first half century of the country's history. This status reflected a much different understanding of abortion at the time, as the word was used during the period only to refer to ending a pregnancy after the "quickening" (well into the second trimester). It also reflected a cultural consensus that issues of reproduction and childbearing were the province of the private home and of women, rather than of public policy and of men. This began to change, however, during the nineteenth century. An extended period of rapid immigration created demographic anxiety among the native-born population about differential birthrates. An urban, industrial economy also commodified and advertised abortion services in ways that offended widespread Victorian attitudes that shunned open discussion of both sexuality and women's health. These concerns led to almost a century of public silence on abortion brought on by the criminalization of the procedure in the last half of the 1800s. Abortion became a taboo topic – even as women continued to seek it and physicians continued to perform it.

After World War II, however, the meaning of abortion began to shift again. Now, increasing medical knowledge contradicted the original arguments made for criminalization. The growing social stature of physicians led them to see the previous century's legal regulations as encroaching on their medical knowledge and clinical autonomy. A far more urbanized and industrialized country led to a population increasingly interested in the timing and number of children they bore. And renewed demographic anxieties, this time brought on by the increased salience of racial conflict, colored people's understanding of the issue.

Chapter 3 revealed the dynamics between the pro-life and pro-choice movements that mobilized around the abortion issue after the 1973 Supreme Court decisions that legalized abortion nationwide. Their origins can be traced back more than a half century. Both movements reflect the divides in the country that have given abortion a wide range of different meanings over time. But the movements have also shaped those meanings. They have actively worked to persuade others of their respective causes, drawing on a range of different social and cultural issues. They have at times drawn on longstanding divisions between Catholics and Protestants. More recently, they have drawn on divisions between more and less "religious" Americans. And the issue of women and their role in society has become central. Both movements have worked tirelessly either to coopt or discredit the persuasive efforts of the other side. And they have done so in a wide variety of venues, from hospitals to churches, from legislative chambers to the courts, to schools and the larger arena of public opinion more generally. The dynamics of their conflict have played a critical role in how abortion is understood today. Neither movement speaks with a single voice, but they have fueled each other, radicalized each other, and kept the issue in the public eye for several generations even as internal fragmentation and division have hampered both movements at key points in their history.

Chapter 4 documents the way in which attitudes toward abortion reflect the layered meanings of the issue. Most Americans have mixed feelings about abortion and do not support the ultimate goal of either movement, abortion whenever a woman wants it, at all stages of pregnancy in the case of the pro-choice movement, or the banning of abortion no matter what the circumstances in the case of the pro-life movement. The vast majority of Americans call themselves either "pro-life" or "pro-choice," but in doing so they mean something different from the activists' views in the movements that bear those labels. The general population is certainly divided on the question, but there is a general consensus that abortions should be permissible in some but not all circumstances. People vary in where they would draw that line, and for many people the line itself is a fuzzy one. In understanding the debate, Americans read into it issues of sexuality, the rights of women, the state of medical knowledge, the role of government, the place of religious faith in their own lives and the lives of their community, and economic and racial anxieties. Despite dramatic changes in overall public attitudes toward a wide variety of different social issues over the last several decades, from homosexuality and premarital sex to capital punishment and drug use, it is a remarkable testament to the permanence of these different social divides that public opinion about abortion has changed very little in almost a half century.

And perhaps no divide is more important to the meaning abortion holds today than the partisan political divide between the Republican and Democratic Parties. Chapter 5 demonstrates the way in which the abortion issue has intersected with American political development. The importance of abortion stems less from its ability to sway the outcome of elections as a voting issue and more from the way it has become a core concern around which each party is organized and defines itself. Abortion was not a partisan issue when it first became an issue of wide public interest. Democrats and Republicans could be found on both sides throughout the 1980s. Nor was it always clear which party would come to adopt which side of the debate. Republicans were actually *more* supportive of abortion rights than Democrats in the years immediately following the *Roe v. Wade* and *Doe v. Bolton* Supreme Court decisions in 1973. Beginning in the 1980s, however, political operatives on both sides worked actively to tie the pro-life and pro-choice movements to the respective political parties. Today, the Republican Party fully embraces the pro-life movement as the Democratic party does the pro-choice movement. This has come at a time when both parties are more ideologically driven and further apart than at any point in American history since the Civil War. The result is that personal identity and under-standings of "us" and "them" have become increasingly tied to identities. And abortion sits at the core of those identities. Views on abortion have come to be more than just opinions – they define a person's character.

People in the rest of the world are divided on the abortion issue, too. The same arguments made by the pro-life and pro-choice movements in the United States are made throughout the world. But abortion is far more culturally and politically central in the US than elsewhere. The controversy permeates American social and political life, while in other places it is largely a settled issue that is seldom the focus of sustained public concern or debate despite continued differences in opinion. Chapter 6 establishes the key factors that make the abortion debate in the United States excep-tional. The institutional structure of the United States, with its fragmented government and weak two-party system, prevents the pro-life or pro-choice movement from scoring decisive political victories and (finally) settling the issue. The transformation of abortion from a technical or medical one to a moral one made compromise more difficult and brought abortion into a long American tradition of moral politics as a substitute (and sometimes proxy) for social class conflict. The exceptional religiosity of Americans has sustained the moral concerns surrounding the issue in ways that proved more difficult elsewhere. So has the malleability of the meaning of abortion, which has been an empty vessel into which various people and interest groups poured their particular concerns and anxieties over time. This morphing of meaning has sustained the red hot passion around abortion in the US at the same time as controversy over the issue cooled in most other places around the world.

## *Where Are We Going?*

The history of abortion in the United States also suggests that the current state of controversy – the increasingly stark difference between the two sides, the increasingly simplistic way in which the issue is discussed publicly, the expectation that everyone will have a strong opinion about the issue tied to their personal and collective identities – does not necessarily define what the abortion debate will look like in the future. If there is a common theme among the different aspects of the debate covered here, it is that the terrain of the abortion controversy is always shifting. So what will it look like five or ten or fifty years from now?

We should always be wary of predicting the future. Social scientists are not prognosticators. Our tools for understanding historical, social, cultural, economic, and political dynamics are all partial and imperfect. Predictions are thus difficult. But there are other reasons to be modest in our claims. Social systems are extremely complicated. We have much to learn about the staggering complexity of the world in virtually all fields of science, but our lack of knowledge is particularly acute, and particularly difficult to improve, when the focus is on human societies. Second, there is always the issue of human agency lurking behind any predictions in the social sciences. Human beings are not atoms, or dollars, or proteins; they have minds of their own and act in ways that are patterned but ultimately not entirely predictable. We therefore do not know what some future pro-life or pro-choice activist, some politician, some physician, some theologian, or some other person might say or do that could change the course of the abortion debate in the future.

Despite these caveats, we can at least define the range of possibilities for the controversy's future. The past and present dynamics of the abortion debate certainly can help us to understand the broad contours that debate will take. The goal is not to choose sides by predicting whether the pro-life or pro-choice movement will win – that is far too simplistic (and also too easy: neither will win). Instead, we should focus on the long-term patterns that have defined the debate across the different topics discussed in the six previous chapters and consider how those patterns are likely to evolve and impact people, organizations, and the wider culture in the future.

First, and most obviously, the meaning of abortion has changed over time. This is the core argument of the book. Abortion has been about issues ranging from the professional expertise of doctors to women's rights, from the impact of immigration to the status of racial conflict, from the importance of religious faith to the role of government in individual lives. It has at times been a medical issue, a legal issue, a technical issue, and a moral issue. The changing meaning of abortion suggests its meaning is likely to continue to change in the future. As medicine and healthcare become increasingly central to public (and political) discussion, perhaps the pro-life and pro-choice sides will come to represent different sides of larger concerns about those subjects. The understanding people have of abortion might be defined by divisions over whether and how proper medical care should be provided to all Americans. The advance of medical technology has already had an important impact on the abortion debate, as the abortion procedure has become medically safer than child-birth (as pro-choice activists will point out) at the same time as medical imaging technology such as ultrasounds have provided visual evidence of the humanity of the developing fetus (as pro-life activists have used to great advantage). Perhaps abortion will in the future come to have meaning in debates over technological advancements such as cloning, gene therapies, and so forth.

Second, the controversy over abortion has seldom focused on the details of the procedure itself. Instead, it has stood in for social divisions of public and private concern, whether they are focused on doctors or women or immigrants or racial minorities or the religious faithful or anyone else. The abortion debate of the future is thus likely to continue to be based on such social divisions. Certainly the social divisions of the past will continue to have salience in the future, particularly divisions over the status of women in society and the proper place of religious faith in public policy. But what new divisions might come to define the abortion debate? Growing inequality is certainly one possibility. Women who receive abortions today, for example, are more likely to be poor and racial minorities than in the past. Also, the influence of globalization and the transformation of the economy may have an effect. Even if we can identify such faultlines, it would be difficult to predict how they will map on to the debate over abortion. Just as it would have been hard to predict which political party would become pro-life and which pro-choice in 1973, so too is it difficult to know precisely how, say, anxieties over inequality will translate into support for one side or the other in the battle over abortion.

Third, the mobilization of the pro-choice and pro-life movements has been critical to sustaining the ongoing abortion controversy. In each chapter, we have seen how the movements played instrumental roles in focusing attention on abortion and connecting the abortion issue to other public concerns as they arose. But much of these efforts came in the early stages of each movement's mobilization. Chapter 3 in particular highlights the dynamism and rapid change among both pro-life and pro-choice organizations and activists in the years surrounding the 1973 Supreme Court decisions. Today, by contrast, both movements are much more mature, and the organizations that lead each – the NRLC and CPCs in the pro-life movement; NARAL, NOW, and Planned Parenthood in the pro-choice movement – are now well-established groups whose outlook and approach are relatively static. They take on new initiatives and fund new campaigns, but otherwise operate in the same way, with the same ideas, year after year. Today, the movements continue to reflect and, at times, selectively amplify, trends and concerns in the larger society, but they are not leading those trends. They are thus unlikely to be major sources of change in the abortion controversy in the future without some major external shock that shakes up one or the other movement, or dramatically changes the social or political terrain on which the battle over abortion is fought.

Fourth, the abortion issue is poised to have a major effect on the evolution of the Democratic and Republican Parties. Much of the analysis here has demonstrated the ways in which external forces in society have impacted the abortion controversy and given it different meanings. But the issue itself has become so ubiquitous, and so important to American politics, that it in turn may have a major effect on the evolution of those politics. We saw hints of this in Chapter 4, where particular beliefs about the abortion procedure itself were less important to people's views than what the issue "represented." Abortion attitudes are increasingly connected to individual and collective identity. This same theme emerged in Chapter 5, which showed how the pro-life and pro-choice causes had become central pillars of the Republican and Democratic Parties. Given this position, abortion has the possibility of shaping the future of politics in the same way that race and racial conflict have shaped, and in many ways dominated, American politics over the last century. Abortion has moved from being one of many social issues to being a core divide in itself within American society and politics.

## What This All Means

The focus of this book has been on understanding abortion politics. But in doing so, the analysis here has inevitably touched on larger issues of how society is organized. In particular, a repeated theme across all the chapters has been the overlapping relationship between beliefs, social structures, and social movements for change. Beliefs are ideas or principles that people, either individually or collectively, hold to be true or important. Certainly beliefs remain at the center of most discussions of abortion, as they continue to revolve around ideas about the procedure and principles that are at stake in either restricting it or making it more available. Social structures are those patterned sets of relationships and expectations that define the way in which people live their individual and collective lives. As we have seen, abortion has become an important element in many social structures, from the provision of medical care to the role of churches, from the status of women in society to the constitution of the major political parties. Social movements are organized attempts to change society, by changing both beliefs and social structures. The abortion issue has led to two of the largest, most well-mobilized, and most well-financed social movements of the twentieth century: the pro-life movement and the pro-choice movement.

The dynamics of abortion politics in the United States show that the relationship between beliefs, social structures, and social movements is an intricate one. As social movements, pro-life and pro-choice activists and organizations have tried to change people's beliefs about abortion and the social structures that control the abortion procedure. But, at the same time, those movements are themselves defined and shaped by the beliefs and social structures that they are confronting. Beliefs are an important starting point for movements, but movements also help define beliefs, particularly the meanings beliefs have for people and the implications they see of those beliefs for the larger society.

This book began by re-telling two minor controversies centered on abortion, one involving Congressman Todd Akin and the other Dr. Kermit Gosnell. They are just two examples of the dozens of incidents of abortion taking center stage in American public discussion. There will certainly be no shortage of additional controversies, both large and small, in the near future. Ultimately, the reason abortion has come to be such a frequent and resonant touchstone for so many social and political controversies is precisely because of the complex, multi-layered set of meanings the issue has taken on over the course of its history. The battle over abortion is in fact a series of different battles over the most important and pressing divides in society. As such, the controversies surrounding it are unlikely to lessen any time soon.

# References

Abramowitz, Alan. 2011. "Partisan Polarization and the Rise of the Tea Party Movement." Retrieved March 16, 2017 (https: //papers.ssrn.com/sol3/papers.cfm?abstract_id=1903153).

Adamczyk, Amy. 2009. "Understanding the Effects of Personal and School Religiosity on the Decision to Abort a Premarital Pregnancy." *Journal of Health and Social Behavior* 50(2): 180–95.

Adams, Greg D. 1997. "Abortion: Evidence of an Issue Evolution." *American Journal of Political Science* 41(3): 718–37.

Amenta, Edwin. 2006. *When Movements Matter: The Townsend Plan and the Rise of Social Security*. Princeton, NJ: Princeton University Press.

American Medical Association. 2017. *2017 AMA Legislative and Regulatory Dashboard*. Retrieved March 16, 2017 (https: //www.ama-assn.org/sites/default/files/media-browser/public/government/advocacy/2017-ama-advocacy-dashboard.pdf).

Andrews, Kenneth T. 2002. "Movement–Countermovement Dynamics and the Emergence of New Institutions: The Case of 'White Flight' Schools in Mississippi." *Social Forces: A Scientific Medium of Social Study and Interpretation* 80(3): 911–36.

Arceneaux, Kevin and Stephen P. Nicholson. 2012. "Who Wants to Have a Tea Party? The Who, What, and Why of the Tea Party Movement." *PS, Political Science & Politics* 45(4): 700–10.

Armstrong, Elizabeth A. 2002. *Forging Gay Identities: Organizing Sexuality in San Francisco, 1950–1994*. Chicago: University of Chicago Press.

Armstrong, Elizabeth A. and Mary Bernstein. 2008. "Culture, Power, and Institutions: A Multi-Institutional Politics Approach to Social Movements." *Sociological Theory* 26(1): 74–99.

Associated Press. 2013. "Abortion Doctor Kermit Gosnell Found Guilty of Murder." *Guardian*, May 13. Retrieved March 16, 2017 (http: //www.theguardian.com/world/2013/may/13/kermit-gosnell-found-guilty-murder).

# References

Back, Kurt W. 1987. "Why Is Abortion a Public Issue? The Role of Professional Control." *Politics & Society* 15(2): 197–206.

Baird-Windle, Patricia and Eleanor J. Bader. 2001. *Targets of Hatred: Anti-Abortion Terrorism*. New York: Palgrave.

Banaszak, Lee Ann and Heather L. Ondercin. 2016. "Explaining the Dynamics between the Women's Movement and the Conservative Movement in the United States." *Social Forces* 95(1): 381–409.

Bartels, Lynn. 2014. "Mark Udall's First Campaign Ad Goes After Cory Gardner on Birth Control, Abortion." *Denver Post*, April 22. Retrieved March 16, 2017 (http://blogs.denverpost.com/thespot/2014/04/22/mark-udall-cory-gardner-ad-birth-control/108396/).

Bean, Lydia. 2014. *The Politics of Evangelical Identity: Local Churches and Partisan Divides in the United States and Canada*. Princeton, NJ: Princeton University Press.

Beckwith, Ryan Teague. 2015. "Transcript: Full Text of the Second Republican Debate." *TIME*. Retrieved March 16, 2017 (http: //time.com/4037239/second-republican-debate-transcript-cnn/).

Beisel, Nicola and Tamara Kay. 2004. "Abortion, Race, and Gender in Nineteenth-Century America." *American Sociological Review* 69(4): 498–518.

Bennard, Kristina Silja. 2005. *The Confirmation Hearings of Justice Ruth Bader Ginsburg: Answering Questions While Maintaining Judicial Impartiality*. American Constitution Society for Law and Policy. Retrieved March 16, 2017 (https: //www.acslaw.org/sites/default/files/Bennard_re_Ginsburg_confirmation_hearings.pdf).

Bernstein, Mary. 2005. "Identity Politics." *Annual Review of Sociology* 31(1): 47–74.

Bernstein, Phylis. 1975. "Anti-Abortion Candidate for President." *New York Times*, November 30.

Blanchard, Dallas A. 1994. *The Anti-Abortion Movement and the Rise of the Religious Right: From Polite to Fiery Protest*. New York: Twayne Publishers.

Blanchard, Dallas A. and Terry J. Prewitt. 1993. *Religious Violence and Abortion: The Gideon Project*. Gainesville: University Press of Florida.

Blank, Rebecca M., Christine C. George, and Rebecca A. London. 1996. "State Abortion Rates: The Impact of Policies, Providers, Politics, Demographics, and Economic Environment." *Journal of Health Economics* 15(5): 513–53.

Boyle, Elizabeth H., Minzee Kim, and Wesley Longhofer. 2015. "Abortion Liberalization in World Society, 1960–2009." *American Journal of Sociology* 121(3): 882–913.

Bremer, Francis J. 2003. *John Winthrop: America's Forgotten Founding Father*. New York: Oxford University Press.

Brodie, Janet Farrell. 1994. *Contraception and Abortion in Nineteenth-Century America*. Ithaca, NY: Cornell University Press.

Brown, Lesley, ed. 1993. *The New Shorter Oxford English Dictionary*. Oxford: Oxford University Press.

Burns, Gene. 2005. *The Moral Veto: Framing Contraception, Abortion, and Cultural Pluralism in the United States*. Cambridge: Cambridge University Press.

Byrnes, Timothy A. 1993. "The Politics of the American Catholic Hierarchy." *Political Science Quarterly* 108(3): 497–514.

Campbell, David E. 2006. "A House Divided? What Social Science Has to Say About the Culture War." *William & Mary Bill of Rights Journal* 15(1): 59–74.

Carless, Will. 2016. "A New Bill Aims to Make Brazil's Abortion Law Even Tougher." *Public Radio International*, March 26. Retrieved March 16, 2017 (https://www.pri.org/stories/2016-03-26/new-bill-aims-make-brazils-abortion-law-even-tougher).

Carmines, Edward G., Jessica C. Gerrity, and Michael W. Wagner. 2010. "How Abortion Became a Partisan Issue: Media Coverage of the Interest Group–Political Party Connection." *Politics & Policy* 38(6): 1135–58.

Carmines, Edward G. and James A. Stimson. 1989. *Issue Evolution: Race and the Transformation of American Politics*, repr. edn. Princeton, NJ: Princeton University Press.

Chesterton, Gilbert Keith. 1922. *What I Saw in America*. London: Hodder and Stoughton, Limited.

Clemens, Elisabeth S. 1997. *The People's Lobby: Organizational Innovation and the Rise of Interest Group Politics in the United States, 1890–1925*. Chicago: University of Chicago Press.

Condit, Celeste. 1994. *Decoding Abortion Rhetoric: The Communication of Social Change*. University of Illinois Press.

Converse, Philip E. 1964. "The Nature of Belief Systems in Mass Publics." In *Ideology and Discontent*, A. D., ed. New York: Free Press, pp. 206–61.

Cook, Elizabeth Adell, Ted G. Jelen, and Clyde Wilcox. 1992. *Between Two Absolutes: Public Opinion and the Politics of Abortion*. Boulder, CO: Westview Press.

Cook, Elizabeth Adell, Ted G. Jelen, and Clyde Wilcox. 1993. "Measuring Public Attitudes on Abortion: Methodological and Substantive Considerations." *Family Planning Perspectives* 25(3): 118–21, 145.

Cook, Philip J., Allan M. Parnell, Michael J. Moore, and Deanna Pagnini. 1999. "The Effects of Short-Term Variation in Abortion Funding on Pregnancy Outcomes." *Journal of Health Economics* 18(2): 241–57.

Cowan, Sarah K., Lawrence L. Wu, Susanna Makela, and Paula England. 2016. "Alternative Estimates of Lifetime Prevalence of Abortion from Indirect Survey Questioning Methods." *Perspectives on Sexual and Reproductive Health* 48(4): 229–34.

Craig, Barbara Hinkson and David M. O'Brien. 1993. *Abortion and American Politics*. Chatham, NJ: Chatham House Publishers.

# References

Critchlow, Donald. 1999. *Intended Consequences: Birth Control, Abortion, and the Federal Government in Modern America*. New York: Oxford University Press.

Critchlow, Donald T. 2007. *The Conservative Ascendancy: How the GOP Right Made Political History*. Cambridge, MA: Harvard University Press.

Darsey, James. 1999. *The Prophetic Tradition and Radical Rhetoric in America*. New York: New York University Press.

Day, Kristen. 2006. *Democrats for Life: Pro-Life Politics and the Silenced Majority*. Portland, OR: New Leaf Publishing Group.

De Tocqueville, Alexis. 2009 [1835]. *Democracy in America*, H. Reeve, ed. Auckland, NZ: The Floating Press.

Diamond, Sara. 1989. *Spiritual Warfare: The Politics of the Christian Right*. Boston: South End Press.

Diamond, Sara. 2000. *Not by Politics Alone: The Enduring Influence of the Christian Right*. New York: Guilford Press.

Dillard, Maria K. 2013. "Movement/Countermovement Dynamics." in *The Wiley-Blackwell Encyclopedia of Social and Political Movements*, D. A. Snow, D. Della Porta, B. Klandermans, and D. McAdam, eds. New Jersey: Blackwell Publishing Ltd.

DiMaggio, Paul, John Evans, and Bethany Bryson. 1996. "Have Americans' Social Attitudes Become More Polarized?" *American Journal of Sociology* 102(3): 690–755.

Doan, Alesha. 2007. *Opposition and Intimidation: The Abortion Wars and Strategies of Political Harassment*. Ann Arbor: University of Michigan Press.

Doherty, Carroll, Jocelyn Kiley, and Bridget Johnson. 2016. *2016 Campaign: Strong Interest, Widespread Dissatisfaction*. Pew Research Center. Retrieved March 16, 2017 (http: //assets.pewresearch.org/wp-content/uploads/sites/5/2016/07/07-07-16-Voter-attitudes-release.pdf).

Dolan, Jay P. 2003. *In Search of an American Catholicism: A History of Religion and Culture in Tension*. Oxford: Oxford University Press.

Donohoe, Martin. 2005. "Increase in Obstacles to Abortion: The American Perspective in 2004." *Journal of the American Medical Women's Association* 60(1): 16–25.

Dubow, Sara. 2010. *Ourselves Unborn: A History of the Fetus in Modern America*. New York: Oxford University Press.

Ehrlich, Sean D. 2011. *Access Points: An Institutional Theory of Policy Bias and Policy Complexity*. New York: Oxford University Press.

Epstein, Leon D. 1986. *Political Parties in the American Mold*. Madison: University of Wisconsin Press.

Esch, Jim. 2017. "The Race for City Council – East Side." *The Reader*, March 30. Retrieved March 16, 2017 (http: //thereader.com/news/the-race-for-city-council/).

Evans, John H., Bethany Bryson, and Paul DiMaggio. 2001. "Opinion

# References

Polarization: Important Contributions, Necessary Limitations." *American Journal of Sociology* 106(4): 944–59.

Fagan, Patrick F. and Scott Talkington. 2014. *Demographics of Women Who Report Having an Abortion*. Washington: Marriage & Religion Research Institute.

Ferree, Myra Marx. 2003. "Resonance and Radicalism: Feminist Framing in the Abortion Debates of the United States and Germany." *American Journal of Sociology* 109(2): 304–44.

Ferree, Myra Marx, William Anthony Gamson, Jürgen Gerhards, and Dieter Rucht. 2002. *Shaping Abortion Discourse: Democracy and the Public Sphere in Germany and the United States*. New York: Cambridge University Press.

Finer, Lawrence B. and Mia R. Zolna. 2016. "Declines in Unintended Pregnancy in the United States, 2008–2011." *New England Journal of Medicine* 374(9): 843–52.

Fiorina, Morris P. and Samuel J. Abrams. 2008. "Political Polarization in the American Public." *Annual Review of Political Science* 11(1): 563–88.

Fiorina, Morris P., Paul E. Peterson, Bertram D. Johnson, and William G. Mayer. 2010. *The New American Democracy*. New York: Pearson.

Fligstein, Neil and Doug McAdam. 2012. *A Theory of Fields*. New York: Oxford University Press.

Ford, Matt. 2016. "US Supreme Court Strikes Down Texas Abortion Restrictions." *The Atlantic*, June 27. Retrieved March 16, 2017 (http://www.theatlantic.com/news/archive/2016/06/texas-abortion-supreme-court/484838/).

Franz, Wanda. 2013. "The Psychology of Rape." *Association for Interdisciplinary Research in Values and Social Change* 25(2). Retrieved March 16, 2017 (http://www.lifeissues.net/writers/air/air_vol25no2_2013.html).

Freeman, Jo. 1973. "The Origins of the Women's Liberation Movement." *American Journal of Sociology* 78(4): 792–811.

Freeman, Jo. 1975. *Politics of Women's Liberation*. New York: Longman Group.

Freidson, Eliot. 1970. *Professional Dominance: The Social Structure of Medical Care*. New Brunswick, NJ: Transaction Publishers.

Fried, Marlene Gerber. 1998. "Abortion in the United States – Legal but Inaccessible." In *Abortion Wars: A Half Century of Struggle, 1950–2000*, ed. R. Solinger, pp. 208–26. Berkeley: University of California Press.

Friedersdorf, Conor. 2013. "Why Dr. Kermit Gosnell's Trial Should Be a Front-Page Story." *The Atlantic*, April 12. Retrieved April 5, 2017 (http://www.theatlantic.com/national/archive/2013/04/why-dr-kermit-gosnells-trial-should-be-a-front-page-story/274944/).

Gallup. 2016a. "Abortion (In Depth: Topics A to Z)." *Gallup*. Retrieved March 16, 2017 (http://www.gallup.com/poll/1576/abortion.aspx).

Gallup. 2016b. "Religion (In Depth: Topics A to Z)." *Gallup*. Retrieved March 16, 2017 (http://www.gallup.com/poll/1690/religion.aspx).

## References

Gallup, George. 1962. "Mrs. Finkbine Gets Confident Vote." *St. Petersburg Times*, October 1, 11 – A.

Gamson, William. 1990 [1975]. *The Strategy of Social Protest*. Belmont, CA: Wadsworth Publishing Company.

Garrow, David J. 1998. *Liberty and Sexuality: The Right to Privacy and the Making of Roe v. Wade*. Berkeley: University of California Press.

Gerdts, Caitlin, L. Fuentes, D. Grossman, K. White, B. Keefe-Oates, S. E. Baum, K. Hopkins, C. W. Stolp, and J. E. Potter. 2016. "Impact of Clinic Closures on Women Obtaining Abortion Services After Implementation of a Restrictive Law in Texas." *American Journal of Public Health* 106(5): 857–64.

Gerlach, Luther and Virginia Hine. 1970. *People, Power, Change: Movements of Social Transformation*. New York: MacMillan Publishing Company.

Ginsburg, Faye. 1998a. "Rescuing the Nation: Operation Rescue and the Rise of Anti-Abortion Militance." In *Abortion Wars: A Half Century of Struggle, 1950–2000*, ed. R. Solinger. Berkeley: University of California Press, pp. 227–50.

Ginsburg, Faye. 1998b. *Contested Lives: The Abortion Debate in an American Community*. University of California Press.

Glendon, Mary Ann. 1987. *Abortion and Divorce in Western Law*. Cambridge, MA: Harvard University Press.

Gorman, Michael J. 1998. *Abortion and the Early Church: Christian, Jewish and Pagan Attitudes in the Greco-Roman World*. Eugene, OR: Wipf & Stock Publishers.

Graber, Mark A. 1999. *Rethinking Abortion: Equal Choice, the Constitution, and Reproductive Politics*. Princeton, NJ: Princeton University Press.

Granberg, Donald. 1981. "The Abortion Activists." *Family Planning Perspectives* 13(4): 157–63.

Granberg, Donald and Beth Wellman Granberg. 1980. "Abortion Attitudes, 1965–1980: Trends and Determinants." *Family Planning Perspectives* 12(5): 250–61.

Green, Emma. 2017. "These Pro-Lifers Are Headed to the Women's March on Washington." *The Atlantic*, January 16. Retrieved April 1, 2017 (https: //www.theatlantic.com/politics/archive/2017/01/pro-lifers-womens-march/513104/).

Greenhouse, Linda and Reva B. Siegel. 2011. "Before (and After) *Roe v. Wade*: New Questions About Backlash." *Yale Law Journal* 120: 2028–87.

Guttmacher Institute. 2014. *Facts on Induced Abortion in the United States*. Guttmacher Institute. Retrieved March 16, 2017 (http://www.guttmacher.org/pubs/fb_induced_abortion.pdf).

Guttmacher Center for Population Research Innovation and Dissemination. 2017. "Requirements for Ultrasound." *State Laws and Policies*. Retrieved August 21, 2017 (https: //www.guttmacher.org/state-policy/explore/requirements-ultrasound).

Hafferty, Frederic W. and Donald W. Light. 1995. "Professional Dynamics and the Changing Nature of Medical Work." *Journal of Health and Social Behavior* Extra Issue: 132–53.

Haines, Herbert H. 1988. *Black Radicals and the Civil Rights Mainstream, 1954–1970.* Knoxville: University of Tennessee Press.

Halfmann, Drew. 2003. "Historical Priorities and the Responses of Doctors' Associations to Abortion Reform Proposals in Britain and the United States, 1960–1973." *Social Problems* 50(4): 567–91.

Halfmann, Drew. 2011. *Doctors and Demonstrators: How Political Institutions Shape Abortion Law in the United States, Britain, and Canada.* Chicago: University of Chicago Press.

Haugeberg, Karissa. 2017. *Women against Abortion: Inside the Largest Moral Reform Movement of the Twentieth Century.* Urbana: University of Illinois Press.

Hellmann, Jessie. 2017. "Trump Reinstates Ban on US Funding for Abortion Overseas." *The Hill*, January 23. Retrieved March 16, 2017 (http: //thehill. com/policy/healthcare/abortion/315652-trump-signs-executive-order-reinstating-global-gag-rule-on).

Holmes, Melissa M., Heidi S. Resnick, Dean G. Kilpatrick, and Connie L. Best. 1996. "Rape-Related Pregnancy: Estimates and Descriptive Characteristics from a National Sample of Women." *American Journal of Obstetrics and Gynecology* 175(2): 320–25.

Holt, Mytheos. 2012. "Mike Huckabee Blasts Critics of Todd Akin in Email: 'Code Red.'" *Theblaze.com*, August 24. Retrieved March 16, 2017 (http: //www.theblaze.com/news/2012/08/24/mike-huckabee-blasts-critics-of-todd-akin-in-email-code-red/).

Hout, Michael. 1999. "Abortion Politics in the United States, 1972–1994: From Single Issue to Ideology." *Gender Issues* 17(2): 3–34.

Howley, Patrick. 2013. "NARAL: Gosnell Murders Are 'Result of Antichoice Attacks on Abortion Access.'" *The Daily Caller*, May 15. Retrieved March 16, 2017 (http: //dailycaller.com/2013/05/13/naral-gosnell-murders-are-result-of-antichoice-attacks-on-abortion-access/).

Huang, Jon, Samuel Jacoby, Michael Strickland, and Rebecca K. K. Lai. 2016. "Election 2016: Exit Polls." *New York Times*, November 8. Retrieved March 16, 2017 (https: //www.nytimes.com/interactive/2016/11/08/us/politics/election-exit-polls.html?_r=0).

Huddy, Leonie, Lilliana Mason, and Lene Aarøe. 2015. "Expressive Partisanship: Campaign Involvement, Political Emotion, and Partisan Identity." *American Political Science Review* 109(1): 1–17.

Hull, N. E. H. and Peter Charles Hoffer. 2001. *Roe v. Wade: The Abortion Rights Controversy in American History.* Lawrence: University Press of Kansas.

Hunt, Scott A. and Robert D. Benford. 2004. "Collective Identity, Solidarity, and Commitment." In *The Blackwell Companion to Social Movements*, D. A. Snow, S. A. Soule, and H. Kriesi, eds. Blackwell Publishing Ltd, pp.433–57.

# References

Hunter, James Davison. 1992. *Culture Wars: The Struggle to Control the Family, Art, Education, Law, and Politics in America*. New York: Basic Books.

Hunter, James Davison. 1994. *Before the Shooting Begins: Searching for Democracy in America's Culture War*. New York: Simon & Schuster.

Hunt, Scott A. and Robert D. Benford. 2004. "Collective Identity, Solidarity, and Commitment." In The Blackwell Companion to Social Movements, D. A. Snow, S. A. Soule, and H. Kriesi, eds. Blackwell Publishing Ltd, pp. 433–57.

Inskeep, Steve. 2015. "Shootings Can't Keep Happening, Planned Parenthood President Says," National Public Radio. Retrieved March 1, 2017 (http: // www.npr.org/2015/11/30/457837732/planned-parenthoods-president-on-last-weeks-fatal-shooting-at-a-colorado-clinic).

Ipsos. 2016. "Canadians Among Most Progressive in Endorsing a Women's Right to Choose." Ipsos. Retrieved March 16, 2017 (http: //www.ipsos-na. com/news-polls/pressrelease.aspx?id=7153).

Jackson, Jesse. 1977. "How We Respect Life Is the Over-Riding Moral Issue." *Right to Life News*, January.

Jacobson, Thomas W. and Wm Robert Johnston. 2017. *Abortion Worldwide Report (2017) – Executive Summary*. The Global Life Campaign. Retrieved March 16, 2017 (https: //media.wix.com/ugd/cacd2b_764ee622b1ab4defa7ec 36dbc82288d8.pdf).

Jacoby, Kerry N. 1998. *Souls, Bodies, Spirits: Drive to Abolish Abortion Since 1973*. Westport, CT: Praeger.

Jaffe, Frederick S., Barbara L. Lindheim, and Philip Randolph Lee. 1981. *Abortion Politics: Private Morality and Public Policy*. New York: McGraw-Hill.

Jasper, James. 2008. *The Art of Moral Protest: Culture, Biography, and Creativity in Social Movements*. Chicago: University of Chicago Press.

Jasper, James M. 2011. "Emotions and Social Movements: Twenty Years of Theory and Research." *Annual Review of Sociology* 37: 285–303.

Jatlaoui, Tara C. et al. 2016. "Abortion Surveillance – United States, 2013." *MMWR Surveillance Summary 2016 – Center for Disease Control* 65(SS-12): 1–44.

Jelen, Ted G. and Clyde Wilcox. 2003. "Causes and Consequences of Public Attitudes Toward Abortion: A Review and Research Agenda." *Political Research Quarterly* 56(4): 489–500.

Jerman, Jenna, Rachel K. Jones, and Tsuyoshi Onada. 2016. *Characteristics of US Abortion Patients in 2014 and Changes Since 2008*. The Guttmacher Institute. Retrieved March 16, 2017 (https://www.guttmacher.org/sites/default/ files/report_pdf/characteristics-us-abortion-patients-2014.pdf

Joffe, Carole E. 1996. *Doctors of Conscience: The Struggle to Provide Abortion Before and After Roe v. Wade*. Boston: Beacon Press.

Joffe, C. E., T. A. Weitz, and C. L. Stacey. 2004. "Uneasy Allies: Pro-Choice Physicians, Feminist Health Activists and the Struggle for Abortion Rights." *Sociology of Health & Illness* 26(6): 775–96.

# References

Jones, Rachel K. and Jenna Jerman. 2017. "Abortion Incidence and Service Availability in the United States, 2014." *Perspectives on Sexual and Reproductive Health* 1(49). Retrieved March 16, 2017 (http: //onlinelibrary. wiley.com/doi/10.1363/psrh.12015/abstract).

Jones, Rachel K. and Megan L. Kavanaugh. 2011. "Changes in Abortion Rates Between 2000 and 2008 and Lifetime Incidence of Abortion." *Obstetrics and Gynecology* 117(6): 1358–66.

Jones, Rachel K. and Kathryn Kooistra. 2011. "Abortion Incidence and Access to Services in the United States, 2008." *Perspectives on Sexual and Reproductive Health* 43(1): 41–50.

Jones, Rachel K. and Kathryn Kost. 2007. "Underreporting of Induced and Spontaneous Abortion in the United States: An Analysis of the 2002 National Survey of Family Growth." *Studies in Family Planning* 38(3): 187–97.

Jones, Richard E. and Kristin H. Lopez. 2014. *Human Reproductive Biology,* 4th edn. San Diego: Academic Press.

Karrer, Robert N. 2011. "The National Right to Life Committee: Its Founding, Its History, and the Emergence of the Pro-Life Movement Prior to *Roe v. Wade.*" *Catholic Historical Review* 97(3): 527–57.

Keller, Rudi. 2012. "Missouri Right to Life President Writes Impassioned Plea for Support for Akin." *Columbia Daily Tribune,* August 25. Retrieved March 16, 2017 (http: //www.columbiatribune.com/news/between_party_lines/missouri-right-to-life-president-writes-impassioned-plea-for-support/article_9da0eee6-358e-5ec1-9dc8-60109b3af683.html).

Kesselman, Amy. 1998. "Women Versus Connecticut: Conducting a Statewide Hearing on Abortion." In *Abortion Wars: A Half Century of Struggle, 1950-2000,* R. Slinger, ed. Berkeley: University of California Press, pp. 42–67.

Kimport, Katrina. 2016. "Divergent Successes: What the Abortion Rights Movement Can Learn from Marriage Equality's Success." *Perspectives on Sexual and Reproductive Health* 48(4): 221–7.

Kinder, Donald R. 1998. "Opinion and Action in the Realm of Politics." In *Handbook of Social Psychology,* vol. 2, D. Gilbert, S. T. Fiske, and G. Lindzey, eds. New York: Oxford University Press, pp. 778–867.

King, Charles R. 1992. "Abortion in Nineteenth-Century America: A Conflict Between Women and Their Physicians." *Womens Health Issues* 2(1): 32–39.

Kretschmer, Kelsy. 2014. "Shifting Boundaries and Splintering Movements: Abortion Rights in the Feminist and New Right Movements." *Sociological Forum* 29(4): 893–915.

Lader, Lawrence. 1955. *The Margaret Sanger Story and the Fight for Birth Control.* Westport, CT: Greenwood Press.

Lahey, Joanna N. 2014a. "Birthing a Nation: The Effect of Fertility Control Access on the Nineteenth-Century Demographic Transition." *The Journal of Economic History* 74(02): 482–508.

# References

Lahey, Joanna N. 2014b. "The Effect of Anti-Abortion Legislation on Nineteenth Century Fertility." *Demography* 51(3): 939–48.

Lawler, Philip. 1992. *Operation Rescue: A Challenge to the Nation's Conscience.* Huntington, IN: Our Sunday Visitor.

Layman, Geoffrey C. 1999. "'Culture Wars' in the American Party System: Religious and Cultural Change among Partisan Activists Since 1972." *American Politics Quarterly* 27(1): 89–121.

Lo, Clarence. 1982. "Countermovements and Conservative Movements in the Contemporary US." *Annual Review of Sociology* 8(1): 107–34.

Lonsway, Kimberly A., Joanne Archambault, and David Lisak. 2009. "False Reports: Moving Beyond the Issue to Successfully Investigate Ann Prosecute Non-Stranger Sexual Assault." *The Voice* 3(1): 1–11.

Luker, Kristin. 1984. *Abortion and the Politics of Motherhood.* University of California Press.

McCarthy, John D. and Mayer N. Zald. 1977. "Resource Mobilization and Social Movements: A Partial Theory." *American Journal of Sociology* 82(6): 1212–41.

McCarty, Nolan and Boris Shor. 2015. "Partisan Polarization in the United States: Diagnoses and Avenues for Reform." *SSRN.* Retrieved January 18, 2017 (https: //ssrn.com/abstract=2714013).

McKeegan, Michele. 1992. *Abortion Politics: Mutiny in the Ranks of the Right.* New York: Free Press.

McKenna, George. 2006. "Criss-Cross: Democrats, Republicans and Abortion." *The Human Life Review* 32(3–4): 57–79.

MacKenzie, John P. 1973. "Supreme Court Allows Early-Stage Abortions." *The Washington Post*, January 23, A1.

Mansbridge, Jane J. 1986. *How We Lost the ERA.* Chicago: University of Chicago Press.

Margenthaler, Julie A. et al. 2003. "Risk Factors for Adverse Outcomes after the Surgical Treatment of Appendicitis in Adults." *Annals of Surgery* 238(1): 59–66.

Marley, Faye. 1963. "Legal Abortion Safer." *The Science Newsletter* 83(9): 134.

Mason, Lilliana. 2016. "A Cross-Cutting Calm: How Social Sorting Drives Affective Polarization." *Public Opinion Quarterly* 80(Special Issue): 351–77.

Maxwell, Carol J. 2002. *Pro-Life Activists in America: Meaning, Motivation, and Direct Action.* Cambridge: Cambridge University Press.

Mercier, Rebecca J., Mara Buchbinder, and Amy Bryant. 2016. "TRAP Laws and the Invisible Labor of US Abortion Providers." *Critical Public Health* 26(1): 77–87.

Merica, Dan. 2015. "On Women's Health, Clinton Compares Republicans to 'Terrorist Groups.'" *CNN.com*, August 28. Retrieved March 16, 2017 (http: //www.cnn.com/2015/08/27/politics/hillary-clinton-republicans-terrorist-groups/index.html).

Meyer, David S. and Suzanne Staggenborg. 1996. "Movements, Counter-movements, and the Structure of Political Opportunity." *American Journal of Sociology* 101(6): 1628–60.

# References

Micklethwait, John and Adrian Wooldridge. 2004. *The Right Nation: Conservative Power in America*. New York: Penguin Press.

Mohr, James C. 1979. *Abortion in America : The Origins and Evolution of National Policy, 1800–1900*. New York: Oxford University Press.

Mooney, Christopher Z. and Mei-Hsien Lee. 1995. "Legislative Morality in the American States: The Case of Pre-Roe Abortion Regulation Reform." *American Journal of Political Science* 39(3): 599–627.

Moore, Peter. 2016. "Most Americans Back Federal Abortion Funding Ban." *YouGov*, August 12. Retrieved March 16, 2017 (https: //today.yougov.com/ news/2016/08/12/taxation-and-morality/).

Morone, James A. 2004. *Hellfire Nation: The Politics of Sin in American History*. New Haven, CT: Yale University Press.

Mouw, Ted and Michael E. Sobel. 2001. "Culture Wars and Opinion Polarization: The Case of Abortion." *The American Journal of Sociology* 106(4): 913–43.

Mudge, Stephanie L. and Anthony S. Chen. 2014. "Political Parties and the Sociological Imagination: Past, Present, and Future Directions." *Annual Review of Sociology* 40(1): 305–30.

Munson, Ziad. 2009. *The Making of Pro-Life Activists: How Social Movement Mobilization Works*. Chicago: University Of Chicago Press.

Munson, Ziad. 2010. "Mobilizing on Campus: Conservative Movements and Today's College Students." *Sociological Forum* 25(4): 769–86.

NARAL Pro-Choice America and Naral Pro-Choice America Foundation. 2017. *Who Decides? The Status of Women's Reproductive Rights in the United States*. Retrieved March 16, 2017 (https: //www.prochoiceamerica.org/ wp-content/uploads/2017/01/WhoDecides2017-DigitalEdition3.pdf).

National Abortion Federation. 2016. *2015 Violence and Disruption Statistics*. Retrieved March 16, 2017 (http: //5aa1b2xfmfh2e2mk03kk8rsx.wpengine. netdna-cdn.com/wp-content/uploads/2015-NAF-Violence-Disruption-Stats. pdf).

National Right to Life Committee. 2011. *National Right to Life Statement on Charges Against Kermit Gosnell*. National Right to Life Committee. Retrieved March 16, 2017 (http: //www.nrlc.org/communications/releases/2011/release011911/).

Neef, Marian Huss. 1979. "Policy Formation and Implementation in the Abortion Field." University of Illinois at Urbana-Champaign. Retrieved March 16, 2017 (https: //www.ideals.illinois.edu/handle/2142/66684).

Nolte, John. 2013. "Washington Post Abortion Poll Asks Most Misleading Question in History." *Breitbart*. Retrieved August 17, 2016 (http: // www.breitbart.com/big-journalism/2013/07/26/wapo-poll-asks-most-misleading-question-in-history/).

Olasky, Marvin. 1992. *Abortion Rites: A Social History of Abortion in America*. Wheaton, IL: Crossway Books.

Oldfield, Duane Murray. 1996. *The Right and the Righteous: The Christian Right Confronts the Republican Party*. Lanham, MD: Rowman & Littlefield.

# References

Olson, Randal S. 2015. "144 Years of Marriage and Divorce in 1 Chart." *Randalolson.com*. Retrieved February 3, 2016 (http: //www.randalolson. com/2015/06/15/144-years-of-marriage-and-divorce-in-1-chart/).

Østvoll, Eirik, O. Sunnergren, E. Ericsson, C. Hemlin, E. Hultcrantz, E. Odhagen, and J. Stalfors. 2015. "Mortality After Tonsil Surgery, a Population Study, Covering Eight Years and 82,527 Operations in Sweden." *European Archives of Oto-Rhino-Laryngology* 272(3): 737–43.

Paige, Connie. 1983. *The Right-to-Lifers: Who They Are, How They Operate, Where They Get Their Money*. New York: Summit Books.

Paulson, Amanda. 2014. "In Colorado Race, Mark Udall Painted Cory Gardner as Anti-Woman. Did It Backfire?" *The Christian Science Monitor*, October 22. Retrieved March 16, 2017 (http: //www.csmonitor.com/USA/Elections/ Senate/2014/1022/In-Colorado-race-Mark-Udall-painted-Cory-Gardner-as-anti-woman.-Did-it-backfire).

Petchesky, Rosalind Pollack. 1984. *Abortion and Woman's Choice: The State, Sexuality, and Reproductive Freedom*, rev. edn. New York: Longman.

Peterson, Chris L. and Rachel Burton. 2007. *US Health Care Spending: Comparison with Other OECD Countries*. Washington: Congressional Research Service.

Pew Research Center. 2015. *US Public Becoming Less Religious*. Retrieved March 16, 2017 (http: //assets.pewresearch.org/wp-content/uploads/sites/11/2015/ 11/201.11.03_RLS_II_full_report.pdf).

Pew Research Center. 2016. *October 2016 Political Survey Final Topline*. Retrieved March 16, 2017 (http: //assets.pewresearch.org/wp-content/uploads/ sites/11/2017/01/11103235/10-27-16-October-topline-for-release.pdf).

Pierson, Paul and Theda Skocpol, eds. 2007. *The Transformation of American Politics: Activist Government and the Rise of Conservatism*. Princeton, NJ: Princeton University Press.

Pollitt, Katha. 2014. *Pro: Reclaiming Abortion Rights*. New York: Picador.

Potts, Malcolm, Peter Diggory, and John Peel. 1977. *Abortion*. Cambridge: Cambridge University Press.

Prendergast, William B. 1999. *The Catholic Voter in American Politics: The Passing of the Democratic Monolith*. Washington: Georgetown University Press.

Pulliam, Sarah and Ted Olsen. 2008. "Q&A: Barack Obama." *Christianity Today*. Retrieved March 27, 2016 (http: //www.christianitytoday.com/ct/2008/ januaryweb-only/104-32.0.html?allcomments=true&start=1).

Putnam, Robert D. and David E. Campbell. 2010. *American Grace: How Religion Divides and Unites Us*. New York: Simon & Schuster.

Reagan, Leslie J. 1998. *When Abortion Was a Crime: Women, Medicine, and Law in the United States, 1867–1973*. Berkeley: University of California Press.

Reger, Jo. 2002. "Organizational Dynamics and Construction of Multiple Feminist Identities in the National Organization for Women." *Gender & Society: Official Publication of Sociologists for Women in Society* 16(5): 710–27.

# References

Reinhardt, Uwe E. 1988. "Healers and Bureaucrats in the All-American Health Care Fray." In *Technology, Bureaucracy and Health in America*, R. J. Bulger, ed. Iowa City: University of Iowa Press.

Riddle, John M. 1994. *Contraception and Abortion from the Ancient World to the Renaissance*. Cambridge, MA: Harvard University Press.

Risen, James and Judy L. Thomas. 1999. *Wrath of Angels: The American Abortion War*. New York: Basic Books.

Rohlinger, Deana A. 2002. "Framing the Abortion Debate: Organizational Resources, Media Strategies, and Movement–Countermovement Dynamics." *Sociological Quarterly* 43(4): 479–507.

Rohlinger, Deana A. 2006. "Friends and Foes: Media, Politics, and Tactics in the Abortion War." *Social Problems* 53(4): 537–61.

Rohlinger, Deana A. 2015. *Abortion Politics, Mass Media, and Social Movements in America*. New York: Cambridge University Press.

Rosin, Hanna. 2012. "Sexual Freedom and Women's Success." *Wall Street Journal*, March 23. Retrieved March 16, 2017 (http: //www.wsj.com/articles/SB10001424052702304724404577299391480959420).

Ross, Loretta J. 2000. "African-American Women and Abortion." In *Abortion Wars: A Half Century of Struggle, 1950–2000*, R. Solinger, ed. Berkeley: University of California Press, pp. 161–207.

Rubin, Eva R. 1987. *Abortion, Politics, and the Courts: Roe v. Wade and Its Aftermath*. Westport, CT: Greenwood Press.

Saad, Lydia. 2011. "Common State Abortion Restrictions Spark Mixed Reviews." *Gallup*, July 25. Retrieved March 16, 2017 (http: //www.gallup.com/poll/148631/common-state-abortion-restrictions-spark-mixed-reviews.aspx).

Saletan, William. 1998. "Electoral Politics and Abortion: Narrowing the Message." In *Abortion Wars: A Half Century of Struggle, 1950–2000*, R. Solinger, ed. Berkeley: University of California Press, pp. 111–23.

Saurette, Paul and Kelly Gordon. 2016. *The Changing Voice of the Anti-Abortion Movement: The Rise of "Pro-Woman" Rhetoric in Canada and the United States*. University of Toronto Press.

Schlozman, Daniel. 2015. *When Movements Anchor Parties: Electoral Alignments in American History*. Princeton, NJ: Princeton University Press.

Schoen, Johanna. 2005. *Choice and Coercion: Birth Control, Sterilization, and Abortion in Public Health and Welfare*, new edn. Chapel Hill: The University of North Carolina Press.

Sedgh, Gilda, Jonathan Bearak, Susheela Singh, Akinrinola Bankole, Anna Popinchalk, Bela Ganatra, Clémentine Rossier, Catlin Gerdts, Özge Tunçalp, Brooke Ronald Johnson Jr., Heidi Bart Johnson, and Leontine Alkema. 2016. "Abortion Incidence Between 1990 and 2014: Global, Regional, and Subregional Levels and Trends." *The Lancet* 388(10041): 258–67.

Shanahan, Eileen. 1976. "Foe of Abortion Qualifies for US Aid." *New York Times*, February 26.

# References

Shimabukuro, Jon O. 2012. *Abortion: Judicial History and Legislative Response.* Washington: Congressional Research Service.

Sinclair, Barbara. 2006. *Party Wars: Polarization and the Politics of National Policy Making.* Norman: University of Oklahoma Press.

Skocpol, Theda and Vanessa Williamson. 2012. *The Tea Party and the Remaking of Republican Conservatism,* 1st edn. New York: Oxford University Press.

Smith, Christian. 1998. *American Evangelicalism: Embattled and Thriving.* Chicago: University of Chicago Press.

Smith, Gregory A. and Jessica Martínez. 2016. "How the Faithful Voted: A Preliminary 2016 Analysis." *Pew Research Center.* Retrieved February 6, 2017 (http: //www.pewresearch.org/fact-tank/2016/11/09/how-the-faithful-voted-a-preliminary-2016-analysis/).

Smith, Tom W. 2012. *Beliefs about God across Time and Countries.* Illinois: National Opinion Research Center (NORC).

Smith, Tom W., Peter Marsden, Michael Hout, and Jibum Kim. 2017. "General Social Surveys, 1972–2016." Retrieved June 6, 2017 (http: //gss.norc.org/).

Snow, David A., Robert D. Benford, Holly J. McCammon, Lyndi Hewitt, and Scott Fitzgerald. 2014. "The Emergence, Development, and Future of the Framing Perspective: 25+ Years Since 'Frame Alignment.'" *Mobilization: An International Quarterly* 19(1): 23–46.

Snow, David A., E. Burke Rochford, Steven K. Worden, and Robert D. Benford. 1986. "Frame Alignment Processes, Micromobilization, and Movement Participation." *American Sociological Review* 51: 464–81.

Solinger, Rickie. 1993. "'A Complete Disaster': Abortion and the Politics of Hospital Abortion Committees, 1950–1970." *Feminist Studies* 19(2): 241–68.

Solinger, Rickie, ed. 1998. *Abortion Wars: A Half Century of Struggle, 1950–2000,* 1st edn. Berkeley: University of California Press.

Soper, J. Christopher. 1994. "Political Structures and Interest Group Activism: A Comparison of the British and American Pro-Life Movements." *Social Science Journal* 31(3): 319–34.

Staggenborg, Suzanne. 1986. "Coalition Work in the Pro-Choice Movement: Organizational and Environmental Opportunities and Obstacles." *Social Problems* 33(5): 374–90.

Staggenborg, Suzanne. 1994. *The Pro-Choice Movement: Organization and Activism in the Abortion Conflict.* New York: Oxford University Press.

Stansell, Christine. 2010. *The Feminist Promise: 1792 to the Present.* New York: Random House.

Steinmo, Sven. 1989. "Political Institutions and Tax Policy in the United States, Sweden, and Britain." *World Politics* 41(04): 500–35.

Storer, H. R. 1866. *Why Not? A Book for Every Woman.* Lee and Shepherd.

Stormer, Nathan. 2002. *Articulating Life's Memory: US Medical Rhetoric about Abortion in the Nineteenth Century.* Lanham, MD: Lexington Books.

Strickland, Ruth Ann and Marcia Lynn Whicker. 1986. "Banning Abortion: An Analysis of Senate Votes on a Bimodal Issue." *Women & Politics* 6(1): 41–56.

Tarrow, Sidney. 2011. *Power in Movement: Social Movements and Contentious Politics.* New York: Cambridge University Press.

Tatalovich, Raymond. 1997. *The Politics of Abortion in the United States and Canada.* Armonk, NY: M. E. Sharpe.

Taylor, Verta. 1989. "Social Movement Continuity: The Women's Movement in Abeyance." *American Sociological Review* 54(5): 761–75.

Taylor, Verta and Nancy Whittier. 1992. "Collective Identity in Social Movement Communities: Lesbian Feminist Mobilization." In *Frontiers in Social Movement Theory*, A. D. Morris and C. M. Mueller, eds. New Haven, CT: Yale University Press, pp. 104–29.

Thomas, Clive S. 2001. "The United States: The Paradox of Loose Party–Group Ties in the Context of American Political Development." In *Political Parties and Interest Groups: Shaping Democratic Governance*, C. S. Thomas, ed. Boulder, CO: Lynne Rienner Publishers, pp. 79–100.

Tietze, Christopher. 1970. "United States: Therapeutic Abortions, 1963 to 1968." *Studies in Family Planning* (59): 5–7.

Tobin, Harper Jean. 2008. "Confronting Misinformation on Abortion: Informed Consent, Deference, and Fetal Pain Laws." *Columbia Journal of Gender and Law* 17(1). Retrieved March 16, 2017 (https: //ssrn.com/abstract=1174297).

Tribe, Laurence H. 1992. *Abortion: The Clash of Absolutes.* New York: W. W. Norton & Co.

Utts, Jessica and Robert Heckard. 2005. *Statistical Ideas and Methods.* Cengage Learning.

Van Dyke, Nella and Holly J. McCammon. 2010. *Strategic Alliances: Coalition Building and Social Movements.* Minneapolis: University of Minnesota Press.

Van Gelder, Lawrence. 1973. "Cardinals Shocked – Reactions Mixed." *New York Times*, January 23, A1.

Viebeck, Elise. 2013. "Republicans Accuse Broadcasters of Gosnell 'Cover-Up.'" *The Hill*, April 17. Retrieved March 16, 2017 (http: //thehill.com/policy/healthcare/294599-republicans-hit-broadcasters-over-gosnell-cover-up-).

Weinberger, Steven E., Hal C. Lawrence 3rd, Douglas E. Henley, Errol R. Alden, and David B. Hoyt. 2012. "Legislative Interference with the Patient-Physician Relationship." *New England Journal of Medicine* 367(16): 1557–59.

Weingarten, Karen. 2014. *Abortion in the American Imagination: Before Life and Choice, 1880–1940.* New Brunswick, NJ: Rutgers University Press.

Wells, Brooke E. and Jean M. Twenge. 2005. "Changes in Young People's Sexual Behavior and Attitudes, 1943–1999: A Cross-Temporal Meta-Analysis." *Review of General Psychology* 9(3): 249–61.

Wilde, Melissa J. 2013. *Vatican II: A Sociological Analysis of Religious Change.* Princeton, NJ: Princeton University Press.

# References

Wilder, Marcy J. 2000. "The Rule of Law, the Rise of Violence, and the Role of Morality: Reframing America's Abortion Debate." In *Abortion Wars: A Half Century of Struggle, 1950–2000*, R. Solinger, ed. Berkeley: University of California Press, pp. 73–94.

Williams, Daniel K. 2012. *God's Own Party: The Making of the Christian Right*, repr. edn. New York: Oxford University Press.

Williams, Daniel K. 2016. *Defenders of the Unborn: The Pro-Life Movement before Roe v. Wade*. Oxford: Oxford University Press.

Willke, John C. and Barbara Willke. 1997. *Why Not Love Them Both?: Questions & Answers About Abortion*. Cincinnati, OH: Hayes Publishing Company.

Witchel, Alex. 1994. "At Home with: Norma McCorvey; of Roe, Dreams and Choices." *New York Times*, July 28. Retrieved February 18, 2016 (http: // www.nytimes.com/1994/07/28/garden/at-home-with-norma-mccorvey-of-roe-dreams-and-choices.html).

Wolbrecht, Christina. 2000. *The Politics of Women's Rights: Parties, Positions, and Change*. Princeton, NJ: Princeton University Press.

Woodberry, Robert D. and Christian S. Smith. 1998. "Fundamentalism et al.: Conservative Protestants in America." *Annual Review of Sociology* 24(1): 25–56.

Woolley, John and Gerhard Peters. 2016. "Presidential Debate at the University of Nevada in Las Vegas." *The American Presidency Project*. Retrieved March 1, 2016 (http: //www.presidency.ucsb.edu/ws/index.php?pid=119039).

World Values Survey Association. 2016. "World Values Survey Wave 6 2010–2014 Official Aggregate v.20150418." *Aggregate File Producer: Asep/JDS, Madrid Spain*. Retrieved November 30, 2016 (www.worldvaluessurvey.org).

Yamane, David A. 2005. *The Catholic Church in State Politics: Negotiating Prophetic Demands and Political Realities*. Lanham, MD: Rowman & Littlefield.

Young, Lisa. 2000. *Feminists and Party Politics*. Vancouver: UBC Press.

Young, Michael. 2002. "Confessional Protest: The Religious Birth of US National Social Movements." *American Sociological Review* 67(5): 660–88.

Zane, Suzanne, A. A. Creanga, C. J. Berg, K. Pazol, D. B. Suchdev, D. J. Jamieson, and W. M. Callaghan. 2015. "Abortion-Related Mortality in the United States: 1998–2010." *Obstetrics and Gynecology* 126(2): 258–65.

Ziegler, Mary. 2009. "The Framing of a Right to Choose: *Roe v. Wade* and the Changing Debate on Abortion Law." *Law and History Review* 27(2): 281–330.

# Index